A New Look at the Last Things

A New Look at the Last Things

John E. Gore

RESOURCE *Publications* · Eugene, Oregon

A NEW LOOK AT THE LAST THINGS

Copyright © 2011 John E. Gore. All rights reserved. Except for brief quotations in critical publications or reviews, no part of this book may be reproduced in any manner without prior written permission from the publisher. Write: Permissions, Wipf and Stock Publishers, 199 W. 8th Ave., Suite 3, Eugene, OR 97401.

Resource Publications
An Imprint of Wipf and Stock Publishers
199 W. 8th Ave., Suite 3
Eugene, OR 97401
www.wipfandstock.com

ISBN 13: 978-1-61097-645-9

Manufactured in the U.S.A.

All scripture quotations, unless otherwise indicated, are taken from the Holy Bible, New International Version®, NIV®. Copyright ©1973, 1978, 1984 by Biblica, Inc.™ Used by permission of Zondervan. All rights reserved worldwide.

This book is dedicated a number of people who have had a profound influence upon my life.

First, to my parents Jack and Edna Gore who loved me and showed me the reality of Jesus by how they lived. I know that my father, who was an honorary lay pastor and one who "loved the Lord's appearing," would be thrilled and proud that this book has been published.

To Sans Souci Baptist Church (Sydney, Australia) where I grew up, and especially to Stan Goodwin, Andy Bligh, Stan Criss, and Vince Duffy. I am grateful to God that I was influenced by such godly but practical men who showed me by word and example what Christian manhood was all about.

Then there is Wishing Well Acres Baptist Church (Toronto, Canada) and their pastor Dr. Will Whitcombe. I learned from him that intellect and faith should be complementary and that both should enrich our lives. To a special group of friends in the church, especially to Keith and Marguerite Davies and Will and Madeline Walker, I have valued your friendship and the influence you have had on me.

There have been others who have impacted me by their teaching. I acknowledge John Wimber, David Pawson, Charlie Moore, and especially Roger Forster. Roger, I feel honored that you have written the foreword to this book.

Finally, the person I most want to dedicate this book to is Carol, my wife of over 40 years. She has supported me, encouraged me, and given me wise counsel when needed. She is my best friend, and I have enjoyed the journey we have taken together. Carol, I love you dearly, and I am grateful that God brought you into my life.

*For the grace of God that brings salvation has appeared to all men.
It teaches us to say "No" to ungodliness and worldly passions,
and to live self-controlled, upright and godly lives in this present age,
while we wait for the blessed hope—the glorious appearing
of our great God and Savior, Jesus Christ.*

—Titus 2:11–13

Contents

Foreword ix

1 Some Opening Thoughts 1

2 The Intermediate State 9

3 The Second Coming of Christ 27

4 The Great Tribulation and the Antichrist 56

5 Our Resurrection Body 73

6 The Millennium 82

7 Judgment 99

8 Hell 114

9 The New Heaven and New Earth 130

Bibliograpy 139

Foreword

Eschatology, the doctrine or study of the last things, is not currently popular. Hence the publication of *A New Look at the Last Things* by John Gore is not only bold, risking ill-informed criticism, but also timely and salutary, filling the large void in most people's understanding and vision of Christianity's worldview.

The lack of popular yet serious study of our Lord's return and the culmination of this age is due to many factors. First, there is the plethora of bizarre interpretations. These views are passed cheaply around with little critical study. They generally owe more to an overactive imagination than to disciplined searching of the Scriptures. It is perhaps unnecessary to add that a disciple is to discipline his mind, motives, and imagination in order to follow his Master's thinking, not his own. Many people have ignored Jesus' helpful warning and analysis of being a finite human—"you know not the day and the hour." It has been fascinating, if not at the same time dismaying, to see come and go a number of "end of the world" dates in my fifty years of Christian ministry. Some of these dates are based on the dimensions of the Tabernacle of Moses, others on biblical archaeology, and others on the pharaohs' timescales, pyramids, and the movement of the stars. My warning note has generally been, perhaps with a touch of sarcasm, "if you go on thinking up any more dates for Jesus' return he will never come, since he said he will come at an hour which 'you think not.'" If we want his return, we had better stop thinking up dates. When beginning on an extended study of the book of Revelation which comprised approximately eighty commentaries and papers, my first three commentaries told me that the stings in the tails of the scorpions of Rev 9:5 were "Turkish guns pulled, pointing backwards by horses in the 17th Century" or "Mussolini's planes with rear-facing gunners in the 20th Century." But best of all the assertions referred to the Methodist class leaders of the eighteenth century. Would you believe it? My apologies to that fine body of men and women for whom I have the highest regard, but evidently the author of this third book must have suffered some traumatic experience from their hands in his youth. These kinds of interpretations have brought much unnecessary ridicule on the divine scriptures causing many true disciples to retreat into the "simple gospel" mentality to avoid exposing themselves to their fellow creature's disparagement. This is sadly to their loss, since "all Scripture is God breathed and is profitable . . ." (2 Tim 3:16). John's book will amply demonstrate this as he investigates end-time teachings, which sharpen our understanding of the beauty of God's character and stimulate us to fulfill Jesus' teaching more accurately. Also, it will give a vision for God's future and love for the creation he has made.

A second reason for a general demise of second-coming teaching is the dogmatic emphasis that the only reality is the here and now of the consumer society with its instant satisfaction. This downgrades any sense of teleological definition. The sophisticated non-believer cannot bear to define reality in terms of its purpose and future. This is because such concepts would imply the necessity of a person to do the purposing, something which they wish to avoid, in order to dismiss God from the scene. However, this superior attitude affects society, and pressurizes, if not embarrasses, the committed believer, on the grounds of his not living the "real" life of societal action, but escaping into future dreams. Of course our reply is that the future visions define, steer, and determine our actions in the present, and the non-believers claim to superior intellectual or moral ground is not really valid, for our opponents have no basis for making definitions at all. These and the added twentieth-century theological emphasis on "realized eschatology," as good as this school of thought may be in many of its insights, have silenced sincere advocates of eschatological study. Such is now out of fashion. Only good works, it is said, will justify our right to exist. The theology of the tower block, which no doubt is important, takes precedence over views regarding the Millennium. Nonetheless, we assert that our good works, together with sometimes the painful experiences in bringing them about and at other times failures, are but "birth pangs" of a coming golden-age that gives reason to our works, which we are assured will not be lost (Rev 14:13). Rather, they will be secured and meaningful for a future eternity.

Third, because there are a variety of interpretations for a particular text from different schools of thought, which seem to generate more heat than light as they interact and conflict with each other, it is deemed polite and spiritual to avoid arousing disagreeable feeling and even losing friendships of a lifetime. It is better therefore to plead ignorance and, rightly, to advocate love, than arguing to prove one is eschatologically right. Such a pathway leads to never discussing God's truth in case we differ. This is very sad as we lose one of the God-ordained ways of discerning our understanding, which is, as it says in the book of Proverbs 27:17, "iron sharpens iron." So we engage with a friend. Again, if Christians are unable to debate, discuss, and disagree and yet still love one another, little progress has been made on the discipleship road (John 13:35).

Last, though I'm sure there are other factors also, some denominations have calcified their approved eschatological schemes for their workers and to some degree their members, which makes it very difficult for some to stay in such situations while reviewing or challenging the accepted denominational stance.

Let me suggest some categories of folk who will not wish to read John's excellent book:

i. Those who do not wish to have their views disturbed.

ii. Those who do not believe the assertion of the seventeenth century pastor John Robinson, who said, "I believe there is yet more light to break forth from God's word," from the sermon he preached to the Pilgrim Fathers as the Mayflower left for the New World.

iii. Those who think the subjects are too difficult, dangerous, or divisive. (However, you would find here in John's loving, careful, and gracious approach a pleasant and edifying corrective.)

However, it is heartening and true to say that spiritual and scholarly opinion continues to converge to a consensus of convictions and opinions leading to a closer obedience to Christ. This seems the more so as we "see the day approaching" of his return. If you are still on the journey in which the Spirit is leading into all truth, you will love the wisdom and clarification that John humbly and carefully presents. It will contribute to your following him who is the truth and you will find yourself closer to him than when you began. Thank you, John, for your hard work and love for Christ and his church.

Roger T. Forster
Ichthus Christian Fellowship
London, UK
February, 2008

1

Some Opening Thoughts

INTRODUCTION

DURING MY EARLY YEARS in pastoral ministry I would say that I held to a "pan-mill" view of our Lord's return; that is, God is in control and it will all "pan out" (work out) in the end. Part of the reason for this is that I couldn't decide what the Bible taught in regard to the last things; especially the millennium and the events associated with it. However, holding to a "pan-mill" view, or not having any view at all, creates a problem if you are a teacher, for you lack the knowledge to confidently preach on the second coming, as well as other topics that we generally put together under the heading of eschatology.[1] As a result, many pastors avoid the subject altogether.

My early years were totally different, for I was raised in a church that enthusiastically taught Dispensational Premillennialism on a regular basis.[2] We were certain that this was correct and that it was the only viable option for anyone who truly believed in the inspiration of Scripture. A major turning point occurred when my wife and I emigrated to Canada

---

1. The English word "eschatology" comes from the Greek word *eschatos*, meaning "last." Eschatology is therefore a study of the last things. It discusses questions such as, "What happens when we die?" "Is there a final judgment, a heaven and a hell?" "Will Christ return to earth, and if so, how and when?" These topics and more belong to the study of eschatology.

2. Dispensational Premillennialism believes that the return of Christ occurs in two stages that are separated by seven years. The first part is the rapture, when Christ comes for his saints and takes them to heaven, while the second phase occurs when he returns to earth with his saints to destroy Antichrist and begin his millennial reign. During the seven-year period the Antichrist makes a covenant with the Jewish people, but breaks it after three and a half years and unleashes a terrible persecution upon them. Refer to chapter 6 for a fuller discussion on this view.

and attended a church where the pastor was a staunch supporter of biblical inerrancy but held an amillennial view of the second coming. This freed me to examine other views of eschatology without feeling that I was being disloyal to the authority of Scripture.

My aim in this book is to give an overview of what I believe the Bible teaches in regard to eschatology. My prayer is that it will cause you to look at Scripture again and to gain a fresh understanding of what it teaches. I trust that upon completion of reading this book you will be able to articulate a biblical view on the last things and be able to share it with others in a confident manner, even if that view is different to the one I hold.

WHY SHOULD WE STUDY ESCHATOLOGY?

The Western church, or at least the part that I am familiar with, has basically ignored the topic of eschatology and has focused almost exclusively on what happens here and now. The current teaching that highlights the benefits that we have in this life by knowing Jesus was a much-needed correction, for there was a time when the second coming of Christ and heaven and hell were the major emphases of the Bible-believing church. People in that era looked forward to the joy of heaven, but overlooked the fact that Christ had come that they might have life, and life to the full, now. However, the pendulum has swung too far, and we need to preach topics that relate to the last things—not exclusively, but as part of an overall balanced approach to biblical teaching. Let me give you the following reasons for studying eschatology.

- 2 Timothy 3:16–17 reminds us that, "All Scripture is God-breathed and is useful for teaching, rebuking, correcting and training in righteousness, so that the man of God may be thoroughly equipped for every good work." We are therefore impoverished if we ignore a major dimension of biblical teaching.

- It is a spur to evangelism. If we only see Christianity as being relevant in this life then it minimizes the urgency to evangelize; especially in countries that are hostile to the gospel. Why should we preach the gospel to Muslims and call them to follow Jesus as Lord if we know that many of them are going to be fiercely persecuted and even put to death? Part of the answer to this question is that there is life after death, a final judgment, heaven and hell. Love demands that we share the gospel with these people, even though many of them will suffer financial and physical loss.

- It is a tool in evangelism. I recently had the privilege of preaching at a missions conference and chose the topic, "Why Should We Obey the Great Commission?" As I was preparing the sermon, I read testimony after testimony of Muslims who had turned to Christ, and central to many of these testimonies was the assurance of heaven that the Bible gives the followers of Jesus. A number of African pastors who have converted from Islam tell me that Muslims are very interested in paradise (heaven), but that the Qur'an doesn't give them any assurance that they will go there after they die.

- It enriches our own spiritual life. I was amazed as I prepared this material at how it enriched my relationship with God in a way that no other subject did, and this included the teaching material I had prepared on *The Person and Work of Jesus* and *The Person and Work of the Holy Spirit*. I found myself singing hymns that related to heaven and feeling an intimacy with God that was unusual. Reflecting on the return of Christ and other related topics is a source of great encouragement. Note 1 Corinthians 15:58, "Therefore, my dear brothers, stand firm. Let nothing move you. Always give yourselves fully to the work of the Lord, because you know that your labor in the Lord is not in vain."

- It draws our attention to the eternal perspective. It reminds us to live with eternity in view and to create priorities that take this into account.

GOD WILL BRING IT ALL TOGETHER

Eschatology is one subject where Bible-believing Christians have genuine differences, and, therefore, we need to exercise a great deal of love and graciousness towards those who believe that the Bible teaches something different to which we hold. When we talk about the last things we are discussing topics that lay beyond the realm of our experience. The idea of being in eternity with a resurrection body that is incapable of decay and death and is not subject to the present laws of physics is something that we have difficulty grasping. Language is limited in conveying concepts of which we have no experience. For example, explain the beauty of a tropical sunset to a man who has been born blind. How would you do it? He has no concept of color. It doesn't matter how clever you are in describing the colors of a sunset, I am sure it would fall far short of the majesty that we experience when we look at it with our physical eyes. Eschatology is like this; the biblical authors, under the inspiration of the Holy Spirit, had to use language that we can understand to explain something that we have never experienced.

I am totally confident that God will bring it all together so that when we are with him in the new heaven and new earth, and we look back and see what has happened, we will say, "Wow, Scripture was right after all; it was just that our minds could not conceive it happening the way it did."

We know that this is what happened in regard to the first coming of Christ. People generally didn't recognize Jesus as the Messiah because he wasn't acting the way they thought the Old Testament prophecies said he would act. They concentrated on one aspect of prophecy—that the Messiah would be a victorious king who was a physical descendant of David—and totally missed two other aspects, the pre-existing divine son of man and the suffering servant. As a consequence, they didn't recognize Jesus when he came. However, when we look at Christ after the event, we can see how these three strands of prophecy came together in an amazing way.

Let us now examine these threads of prophecy in order to fully appreciate this. First, there is the Davidic king, the one who was the heir to the throne of David. (In New Testament times this person was called the "Messiah," "the Christ," and "the Anointed One".) Isaiah 11 refers to the Messiah and tells how the royal lineage from David would appear to have fallen and be gone forever, but people are not to lose hope, for one day a shoot will appear and an heir of David will take the throne. The Spirit of the Lord will rest upon him and give him wisdom and understanding. He will rule his people Israel with justice and mercy and destroy their enemies: "A shoot will come up from the stump of Jesse; from his roots a Branch will bear fruit. The Spirit of the LORD will rest on him— the Spirit of wisdom and of understanding, the Spirit of counsel and of power, the Spirit of knowledge and of the fear of the LORD—and he will delight in the fear of the LORD. He will not judge by what he sees with his eyes, or decide by what he hears with his ears; but with righteousness he will judge the needy, with justice he will give decisions for the poor of the earth. He will strike the earth with the rod of his mouth; with the breath of his lips he will slay the wicked" (Isa 11:1–4).

There is nothing here about a humble prophet from Nazareth who went around doing good or a pre-existent divine being who became a man. There is nothing about a humble servant who suffered death so he could deal with the sin of mankind. Rather the emphasis is on his victorious rule where he destroys the wicked by his power and introduces a reign of peace and righteousness. One can understand why John the Baptist and Jesus' disciples were puzzled by Jesus' behavior. How could he be the long-awaited Messiah when he was not acting like the victorious earthly king who would free Israel from the oppression of Rome?

The second picture of the Messiah is found in Daniel 7 and is totally different from the Davidic king of Isaiah 11. In his vision Daniel sees a figure "like a son of man" who is a pre-existing divine person who is given an everlasting kingdom and who receives worship from peoples of every nation and language: "In my vision at night I looked, and there before me was one like a son of man, coming with the clouds of heaven. He approached the Ancient of Days and was led into his presence. He was given authority, glory and sovereign power; all peoples, nations and men of every language worshiped him. His dominion is an everlasting dominion that will not pass away, and his kingdom is one that will never be destroyed" (Dan. 7:13–14).

Imagine the confusion of the disciples when Jesus started to use this term. How could he be the divine son of man when everyone knew his parents and brothers and sisters? (Let me digress to say that Jesus used the term "son of man" to teach that he was the heavenly pre-existing divine figure of Daniel 7:14. He quoted this verse at his trial when he was asked if he was the Christ, the Son of the Blessed One. Refer to Mark 14:61–64. The high priest knew that Jesus was claiming to be divine. That is why he described Jesus' answer as blasphemy and worthy of death.)

These two figures, the earthly Davidic king and the heavenly pre-existing divine son of man, seem to be mutually exclusive. How can the Messiah be the earthly heir to the Davidic throne and be a pre-existing divine character?

The third picture of the Messiah is the suffering servant as found in Isaiah 53. This person is humble, passive, and oppressed: "He was oppressed and afflicted, yet he did not open his mouth; he was led like a lamb to the slaughter, and as a sheep before her shearers is silent, so he did not open his mouth" (verse 7). This servant will meet an early death as he suffers for the sins of the people: "But he was pierced for our transgressions, he was crushed for our iniquities; the punishment that brought us peace was upon him, and by his wounds we are healed . . . For he was cut off from the land of the living; for the transgression of my people he was stricken" (verses 5, 8b). At times the servant swings from being Israel as a whole to an individual who redeems Israel. However, looking back we see how Jesus beautifully fulfills the prophecy concerning this suffering servant.

The suffering servant is different from the Davidic king and the pre-existing son of man. How can the Messiah at one and the same time be someone who smites the earth with the rod of his mouth and slays the wicked with the breath of his lips, but also be one who is smitten and passively allows himself to be put to death. How can he be a descendant of the earthly king David but at the same time be a pre-existing divine figure? What seemed impossible to grasp in the Old Testament becomes understandable when we read the New Testament. All of these three concepts find their fulfillment in Jesus who was fully God and fully man of the line of David—the one born in a manger who died for our sin and who will come again as judge of all.

There are many aspects to eschatology that we cannot fully understand now, but we can be confident that when we get to be with God in the new heaven and new earth, we will look back and say, "Wow, Scripture was right after all; it was just that our minds could not conceive of it happening the way it did."

WE START WITH THE NEW TESTAMENT

This study is based on the assumption that the Bible is the inspired infallible word of God, that is without error in all it affirms. Therefore, the Bible is our ultimate source of authority concerning the things that relate to the "end times" and the final state in the "age to come." By ultimate source I mean that we will look at other sources to get insight that helps us to understand the Bible better, but ultimately it is what the Bible says, rightly interpreted, that is our authority on the "last things."

It is my firm belief that we need to develop our understanding of doctrine by asking, "What does the New Testament teach?" Once we have this as our starting point, we can then look back to the Old Testament to gain further understanding and insight. The book of Hebrews tells us that the death and resurrection of Jesus ushered in a new covenant that is superior to the old one: "But the ministry Jesus has received is as superior to theirs as the covenant of which he is mediator is superior to the old one, and it is founded on better promises" (Heb. 8:6). The writer goes on to say that the new covenant introduced by Jesus, which is recorded in the pages of the New Testament, makes the first covenant, as recorded in the pages of the Old Testament, obsolete: "By calling this covenant 'new,' he has made the first one obsolete; and what is obsolete and aging will soon disappear" (Heb. 8:13).

This doesn't mean that the Old Testament is no longer of any value—far from it—for the New Testament says that all Scripture is God-breathed and, in the context, this refers primarily to the Old Testament. What it does mean is that the Old Testament must be interpreted in light of the New Testament. That is, we start with the New Testament and then look back to the Old Testament and interpret it in line with Jesus.

Hebrews 10:1 tells us "the law is only a shadow of the good things that are coming— not the realities themselves." Developing a doctrine by starting with the Old Testament is like trying to discover what something is like by looking at the shadows. We need to look at the reality of the object itself rather than the shadow it casts if we want to have an accurate picture.

A NOTE OF CAUTION

The area of eschatology is one where some people want to know every detail and, in order to satisfy their curiosity, allow their imaginations to run riot and develop elaborate schemes and systems to embellish the clear teaching of Scripture. We should shy away from this approach because there are many things that God doesn't want us to know at this stage. The apostle Paul, who was taken to heaven and given divine insight into many aspects that relate to the future, was not allowed to share all he saw: "And I know that this man—whether in the body or apart from the body I do not know, but God knows—was caught up to paradise. He heard inexpressible things, things that man is not permitted to tell" (2 Cor 12:3–4).[3] However, God has revealed certain things to encourage us and strengthen us as we serve him. For example, in the

---

3. Beasley-Murray, "*2 Corinthians*," 71, writes "In view of the context and the definition of the theme in v. 1, it is not to be doubted that the *man in Christ* of v. 2 is Paul" (Emphasis in original.)

latter part of 1 Corinthians 15, that great chapter that talks about our resurrection body, Paul exhorts the Corinthians to be encouraged and to stand firm in their faith because of the certainty of living with God forever in their resurrection bodies. "Therefore, my dear brothers, stand firm. Let nothing move you. Always give yourselves fully to the work of the Lord, because you know that your labor in the Lord is not in vain" (1 Cor 15:58). A study of eschatology is meant to spur us on to evangelism and holy living.

We need to recognize, as we progress through this study, that godly Bible-believing Christians often interpret the Bible differently in some minor points of eschatology. We must respect and love one another and not brand others as "liberal" or "modernist" simply because they do not interpret Scripture in the same way we do. The fact that Bible-believing Christians can genuinely have different opinions, and the fact that there are many things about the future that God doesn't want us to know at this stage (2 Cor 12:4), should lead us to a position of humility and respect for each other.

OVERVIEW

The following diagram is an overview of what I will be teaching during this book.

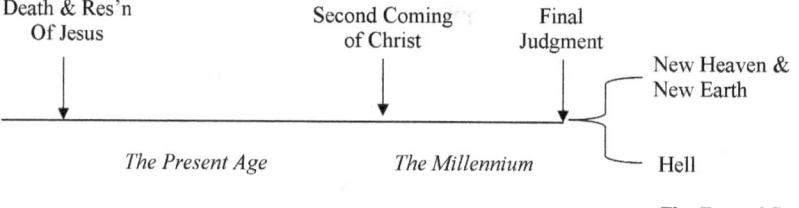

Historic Premillennial View

This is known as the Historic Premillennial view. "Pre" means "before," hence Christ will return before he introduces his millennial reign on earth. The term "Historic" is used to distinguish it from the Dispensational Premillennial view.

2

The Intermediate State

WE ARE MORE THAN A PHYSICAL BODY

The cynic may say, "When you are dead you're dead, 'cause there is nothing after this life!" But this is not what the Bible teaches. There is an immaterial part of man, his inner self, which lives on after physical death.

Consider the following Scriptures:

- Luke 23:43, "Jesus answered him, 'I tell you the truth, today you will be with me in paradise.'" Jesus promised the repentant thief that, even though he was going to die physically that day, his inner person would then be with him in paradise.

- Acts 7:59, "While they were stoning him, Stephen prayed, 'Lord Jesus, receive my spirit.'"

- 2 Corinthians 5:6–9, "Therefore we are always confident and know that as long as we are at home in the body we are away from the Lord. We live by faith, not by sight. We are confident, I say, and would prefer to be away from the body and at home with the Lord. So we make it our goal to please him, whether we are at home in the body or away from it."

- Philippians 1:21–24, "For to me, to live is Christ and to die is gain. If I am to go on living in the body, this will mean fruitful labor for me. Yet what shall I choose? I do not know! I am torn between the two: I desire to depart and be with Christ, which is better by far; but it is more necessary for you that I remain in the body."

Physical death is not the end of man's conscious existence; the inner self lives on.[1]

DEFINITION OF "THE INTERMEDIATE STATE"

We can define the intermediate state as, "The existence of both the righteous and the wicked after death and prior to the resurrection."

The phrase "intermediate state" is not a biblical term but is one developed by theologians to describe the state of a person between physical death and our final state; hence the name "intermediate state." Some people prefer the term "disembodied state," since it is the time when we will not have a body. I prefer the more common term, "the intermediate state." The final state for the believer will be in the new heaven and new earth with our resurrection bodies when we see Christ face to face.

WHY DO BELIEVERS PHYSICALLY DIE?

This is a good question. If death is the result of sin, which it is (Rom 5:12), and if our sin has been forgiven, which it has (Col 2:13), and if believers are not under any condemnation, which they aren't (Rom 8:1), then why do we physically die? To answer this question we must understand the nature of salvation, especially the past, present, and future dimensions. Salvation is not just rescue from sin but rescue from its consequences, with the resulting transformation into the likeness of Jesus.

- Past dimension. Titus 3:5, Colossians 1:13, and John 5:24 tell us that we have been rescued from the kingdom of darkness and brought into the kingdom of Jesus when we believe. We have eternal life and have crossed over from death to life. However, while we have a new status as God's children and belong to his family, we still suffer from the consequences of our sin.

- Present dimension. Refer to 1 Corinthians 1:18 and 2 Corinthians 2:15. We are being saved in that we are being rescued from the consequences of our sin and being transformed into the image of Christ. Our relationship with God is not in doubt, because we have crossed from death to life, but we need to be rescued from sin's consequences.

---

1. For the benefit of this study I will use the terms "soul," "spirit," and "heart" as interchangeable words for our "inner selves" or the "real us."

- Future dimension. Refer to Romans 13:11, 1 Peter 1:5, and Hebrews 9:28. This refers to the complete rescue from the consequences of sin and the total transformation to be like Jesus. It requires us to receive our resurrection bodies and be totally freed from sin and death.

The Bible teaches that our status and eternal destiny are changed the moment we repent and put our trust in Jesus, but the transformation process is a life-long process, plus more. We don't get all the benefits of salvation until we are in the new heaven and new earth with our new resurrection bodies, where sin and death have been banished. Physical death for the believer represents being a step closer to that final state when we are totally freed from the consequences of sin and totally transformed to be like Christ. Physical death means that we are with the Lord in a far more intimate way than we experience now. Death is not a defeat for the believer but a "promotion to glory," as the Salvation Army describes it; it is one step closer to receiving our resurrection bodies and the new heaven and new earth.

This doesn't mean that those who are left should not mourn the death of a loved one who was a believer, but they do not mourn as people who have no hope. In the midst of the sorrow that those who are left behind feel, there is a sense of hope that the believer has gone to be with the Lord and this, for them, is far better: "Brothers, we do not want you to be ignorant about those who fall asleep, or to grieve like the rest of men, who have no hope. We believe that Jesus died and rose again and so we believe that God will bring with Jesus those who have fallen asleep in him" (1Thess. 4:13–14).

In response to the question, "Why does the believer die if his or her sin is forgiven?" part of the answer is found in the fact that salvation has several stages and we don't experience it all at once. If we did, then we would be immediately removed from this sin-affected world and taken to live with God in the new heaven and new earth the moment we believed. Who would be left to do evangelism, if that were the case? Dying is part of the transformation process where we leave our sin-affected physical body behind and go to be in the presence of the Lord in a fuller way. There will be a generation, and I refer to those who will be alive when Christ returns, who will not experience physical death, but will be transformed immediately and receive their resurrection bodies without dying.

WHAT HAPPENS TO A BELIEVER WHEN HE OR SHE PHYSICALLY DIES?

Present With the Lord Upon Death and Aware of It

When the believer dies, his or her soul/spirit is immediately ushered into the presence of the Lord and away from this sin-affected world. He or she experiences an intimacy with God that far surpasses anything he or she has previously known. Consider the following verses:

- Philippians 1:22–25, "If I am to go on living in the body, this will mean fruitful labor for me. Yet what shall I choose? I do not know! I am torn between the two: I desire to depart and be with Christ, which is better by far; but it is more necessary for you that I remain in the body. Convinced of this, I know that I will remain, and I will continue with all of you for your progress and joy in the faith." Paul had a strong desire to depart this world so that he could immediately enjoy being in the presence of God. This is not escapism on the part of Paul, for he really wanted to stay alive physically so that he could preach the gospel, but the appeal of being in the presence of the Lord, in a way beyond what he could experience with the limitations of his earthly body, was so appealing that he found himself in a dilemma: do I go or do I stay? He chose to put aside his desire to be with the Lord so that he could stay in the body and minister further to the Philippians and others.

- Jesus said to the thief on the cross, "Today you will be with me in Paradise" (Luke 23:43). The first-century Jews understood paradise as a place where one experienced great blessing and joy in the presence of God; it was not a state of unconscious existence.[2] This expectation of immeasurable joy in the presence of God explains why Paul wanted to "depart and be with Christ, which is far better." There are some who say that this verse should be translated, "I say to you today, that you will be with me in paradise," meaning that Jesus didn't promise the thief that he would be with him in paradise that day but simply that Jesus spoke the words that day. This has little to commend it, for how can anyone say something except that they say it that day?

---

2. Grudem, *Systematic Theology*, 820.

- 2 Corinthians 5:6–8, "Therefore we are always confident and know that as long as we are at home in the body we are away from the Lord. We live by faith, not by sight. We are confident, I say, and would prefer to be away from the body and at home with the Lord." Paul had a great confidence that when he died he would go straight into the presence of the Lord and enjoy intimate fellowship with him.

There are those, including Martin Luther, who teach that upon physical death the soul/spirit goes to be with God, but is in a state of unconscious existence. The next event that a person's soul/spirit is conscious of is the return of Christ when it awakes from its "sleep" and accompanies him back to earth. This doctrine is known as "soul sleep." The basis of this teaching is usually found in the fact that the Bible often talks about death as "sleep" or "falling asleep." (For example, 1 Corinthians 15:51 reads, "Listen, I tell you a mystery: We will not all sleep, but we will all be changed.") However, to interpret this as meaning that the soul sleeps in a state of unconsciousness upon physical death is to misunderstand the use of the word, for the term "sleep" is meant to convey the concept that death for the believer is not something to be feared, nor is it the end.

For the believer, death has no more fear than going to sleep. It is a temporary and pleasant experience rather than a fearful one for those who are in Christ. We see this in John 11:11, "After he had said this, he went on to tell them, 'Our friend Lazarus has fallen asleep; but I am going there to wake him up.'" John tells us that his disciples didn't realize that Jesus was using sleep as a metaphor for death for they said, "Lord, if he sleeps, he will get better." John continues in verse 13–14, "Jesus had been speaking of his death, but his disciples thought he meant natural sleep. So then he told them plainly, 'Lazarus is dead.'"

When Paul refers to believers who have fallen asleep he is talking about believers who have physically died: "Brothers, we do not want you to be ignorant about those who fall asleep, or to grieve like the rest of men, who have no hope. We believe that Jesus died and rose again and so we believe that God will bring with Jesus those who have fallen asleep in him" (1 Thess. 4:13–14). Sleep is a metaphor for death—something that is temporary and not to be feared.

We noted in Philippians 1:22–25 and 2 Corinthians 5:6–8 that Paul expected to be ushered into the presence of the Lord immediately upon death and to be conscious of it; otherwise his comments do not make sense. If death ushered us into an extended period of unconscious rest then why would he be torn between "wanting to depart and be with Christ" and staying in the body and working with the believers for "their progress and joy in the faith"? If the intermediate state for the believer is only a place of "soul sleep," then Paul would not have been in the dilemma that he was. Paul confidently expected that when he physically died he would go into the presence of the Lord, and that he would be consciously aware of the Lord's presence. He was not looking for a place of rest but conscious intimacy with God.

Experience suggests that Jesus comes for the believer just before physical death and takes them home to be with him. Let me share what happened to two of my aunts. In the days that led up to my Aunty Evelyn's death, she was in the hospital and very sedated. The day she died she didn't move or even open her eyes. (My cousin Heather was with her the whole time.) Later in the day the nurse came to change the morphine drip, and, while she was doing this, Aunty Evelyn, who hadn't moved or even opened her eyes up until then, suddenly sat up with her eyes wide open and was transfixed on something ahead of her, about where the wall met the ceiling. After a short period she lay down, turned her head, looked at her two daughters, and then died. My cousin Heather said that when my Aunt suddenly sat up and opened her eyes and stared up ahead of her, she knew what was happening because Heather, like me, had heard many stories where Christians see something in front of them and then suddenly die. While Aunty Evelyn didn't say anything, I have heard other incidents where the person says that Jesus has come into the room to take them home.

My Aunt Betty had a similar experience. While the nurse was attending her she suddenly looked up towards the top corner of the room and was transfixed by what was happening. The nurse and my cousin tried to get her attention, but they couldn't distract her from what she was seeing. The nurse then walked to the other side of the bed and physically put her body between Aunty Betty and what she was looking at. An instant later Aunty Betty lay down and died. In both these cases we don't know what they saw, but it must have been something like Jesus coming to take them home to cause them to react the way they did. Unfortunately, I didn't see my parents the instant they died. I was with my father at the time, but he walked to the toilet in his home and died there while I was with Mom in the living room. My mother died while I was out of the country, so I don't know if she saw anything a minute or so before she went to be with the Lord.

I believe that the moment a believer dies he is in the presence of the Lord and experience suggests that Jesus comes to them immediately prior to physical death to take them home. I believe that this is what Jesus had in mind when he said, "And if I go and prepare a place for you, I will come back and take you to be with me that you also may be where I am" (John 14:3).

I have sometimes wondered if my Aunts had a similar experience to Stephen who saw "heaven open and the Son of Man standing at the right hand of God" shortly before he died (Acts 7:56). But was this all that Stephen saw, or did he actually see Jesus coming for him immediately before dying, and were the heavens opening simply a precursor to that?

Before I leave this topic I want to discuss the teaching that when a person dies physically he or she is totally dead without any consciousness and he or she stays in that state until the resurrection. This view denies that there is an intermediate or disembodied state where the immaterial part of a person, his or her soul/spirit, is alive. This view understands "body," "soul," and "spirit" as different ways of describing a person and not as separate parts of that person.

In response to this line of thinking we can say that there are verses in Scripture that affirm that our souls or spirits live on after our bodies die. For example:

- Matthew 10:28, "Do not be afraid of those who kill the body but cannot kill the soul. Rather, be afraid of the One who can destroy both soul and body in hell." Jesus draws a distinction here between body and soul and tells us that our bodies can be killed while our souls live on.

- If Paul thought that his soul didn't survive physical death but had to wait until the resurrection before it received consciousness again, why was he in such a dilemma? In Philippians 1:23 he says, "I desire to depart and be with Christ." This verse only make sense if Paul had a rock-like conviction that his soul lived on after physical death, and that he immediately would go into the presence of his Lord in his disembodied state and be aware of it.

However, we need to recognize that the final state of the believer is in the new heaven and new earth with our imperishable resurrection bodies.

The Believer Goes to Heaven (Paradise) Upon Physical Death

It is a marvelous truth that the believer is with the Lord the instant he or she dies, but where does he or she go? We noted above in Luke 23:43 that Jesus promised the repentant thief that he would be in paradise with him that very day. Every time the word "paradise" was used outside of the Bible it referred to a garden or park, a place of beauty and enjoyment. Paradise is another name for heaven. The word is used in 2 Corinthians 12:2–4, "I know a man in Christ who fourteen years ago was caught up to the third heaven. Whether it was in the body or out of the body I do not know—God knows. And I know that this man—whether in the body or apart from the body I do not know, but God knows—was caught up to paradise. He heard inexpressible things, things that man is not permitted to tell." The "third heaven" in verse two is the same as "paradise" in verse four. The NIV Study Bible makes this comment, "The third heaven designates a place beyond the immediate heaven of the earth's atmosphere and beyond the further heaven of outer space and its constellations into the presence of God himself. Thus the risen and glorified Lord is said to have passed 'through the heavens' (Heb. 4:14), and now, having 'ascended higher than all the heavens' (Eph. 4:10), to be 'exalted above the heavens' (Heb. 7:26). The term 'paradise' is synonymous with the third heaven, where those believers who have died are even now 'at home with the Lord.'"[3] The "third heaven" is what we commonly refer to as "heaven," and this is where the believer goes upon physical death.

We can define heaven as, "the place where God's presence is centralized; it is where the risen Lord resides in his resurrection body at the right hand of the Father." While God is omnipresent, in that he is everywhere at the same time, there is a place where his presence is centralized. The angel told the disciples in Acts 1:11 that Jesus had been taken up into heaven and would come again from heaven, so heaven is a place. Furthermore, in Acts 7:55–56, we read that Stephen saw heaven immediately prior to death, "But Stephen, full of the Holy Spirit, looked up to heaven and saw the glory of God, and Jesus standing at the right

---

3. Barker, *NIV Study Bible*, 1776.

hand of God. 'Look,' he said, 'I see heaven open and the Son of Man standing at the right hand of God.'" Heaven is the place where the Son is standing at the right hand of the Father.

It seems that the location of paradise or heaven will change in the future and will be different from what or where it is now. The New Testament tells us that the final dwelling place of the believer will be in the new heaven and new earth. In Revelation 21:1–3 we note that the new heaven and new earth have come into being and that God now dwells with man in this setting. "Then I saw a new heaven and a new earth, for the first heaven and the first earth had passed away, and there was no longer any sea. I saw the Holy City, the new Jerusalem, coming down out of heaven from God, prepared as a bride beautifully dressed for her husband. And I heard a loud voice from the throne saying, 'Now the dwelling of God is with men, and he will live with them. They will be his people, and God himself will be with them and be their God.'" In Revelation 2:1–7 the church at Ephesus was promised that, if they overcame, they would have the right to eat from the tree of life that is in the paradise of God. However, when we next read about the tree of life it is situated in the new heaven and new earth. Refer to Revelation 22:2. Here we see that the final location of paradise, or heaven, is in the new heaven and new earth.

What do we conclude from this? When the believer dies he immediately goes to paradise, what we commonly call heaven, and is in the presence of God in a far more intimate way than he or she has ever experienced before. It is something the apostle Paul looked forward to. Heaven is a definite place, although we should not think of it as necessarily having physical structures as we know them. It is where Jesus is presently at the right hand of the Father. However, the present location of paradise, wherever it may be, is not its final location, for it will shift to the new heaven and new earth, where God will finally dwell with his people.

EXPERIENCING HEAVEN NOW

There is a sense is which we experience heaven now. If we define heaven as "the place where the Son is standing at the right hand of the Father," then there is a part of us that is in heaven now. For, according to Paul, we are seated with Christ in the heavenly realms (Eph. 2:6), and therefore we are, in a small way, experiencing its pleasures now. When we worship

God and get "lost in wonder, love, and praise," this is a foretaste of what heaven is going to be like. However, it is only a foretaste, for our present sinful nature stops us from seeing God face to face. What we now see is but a poor reflection; however, it is a reflection and not something totally different. It is the Holy Spirit within us who gives us this foretaste of what is to come; he is the deposit that guarantees our complete inheritance (2 Cor 5:5; Eph 1:14).

COMMENTS ON 2 CORINTHIANS 5:1–10

> Now we know that if the earthly tent we live in is destroyed, we have a building from God, an eternal house in heaven, not built by human hands. 2 Meanwhile we groan, longing to be clothed with our heavenly dwelling, 3 because when we are clothed, we will not be found naked. 4 For while we are in this tent, we groan and are burdened, because we do not wish to be unclothed but to be clothed with our heavenly dwelling, so that what is mortal may be swallowed up by life. 5 Now it is God who has made us for this very purpose and has given us the Spirit as a deposit, guaranteeing what is to come. Therefore we are always confident and know that as long as we are at home in the body we are away from the Lord. 7 We live by faith, not by sight. 8 We are confident, I say, and would prefer to be away from the body and at home with the Lord. 9 So we make it our goal to please him, whether we are at home in the body or away from it. For we must all appear before the judgment seat of Christ, that each one may receive what is due him for the things done while in the body, whether good or bad. (2 Cor. 5:1–10)

These verses carry on from the end of chapter 4, where Paul talks about the eternal glory that awaits the believer. When our earthly tent, that is, our physical body, is destroyed, we know that this is not the end, for God has prepared a house in heaven for us. Some want to see this "eternal house in heaven" as referring to our resurrection body, and while a case can be made for that, I do not think Paul is referring to this. I believe Jesus' words in John 14 form the basis for Paul's thoughts here. Jesus told his disciples that he was going away to prepare a place for them in heaven:[4] "In my Father's house are many rooms; if it were not so, I would have told you. I am going there to prepare a place for you" (John 14:2).

---

4. Morris, *The Gospel According to John*, 638. Commenting on verse 2 Morris writes, "My Father's house clearly refers to heaven."

When Paul talks about "an eternal house in heaven," he is looking forward to being immediately transported into the presence of God when he physically dies, and inhabiting the "mansion" that has been prepared for him.

Allow me to digress and say that I don't believe either Jesus or Paul intend for us to understand John 14:2 and 2 Corinthians 5:2 respectively, as referring to a physical structure made out of bricks and timber, but rather a "home" for us in paradise in the presence of God. Why would we require a physical building made of bricks and timber when we do not have a physical body in our intermediate state? However, the idea of a "home" conjures up a picture of security, protection, warmth, somewhere to belong, something to call our own, a place of hospitality, and joy. When Jesus says that he is going to prepare a place for us, he is using human language that we understand to convey truths that we can't understand. We can't conceive of living without a physical body and so we can't grasp what God has in store for us. Human language is inadequate to describe spiritual concepts because we have nothing with which to compare them. It is like trying to explain the beauty of a tropical sunset to a person who was born blind. However, the idea of a house that Jesus is preparing for us helps us to appreciate the wonder of what God has planned for those who love him. We know that when we die Jesus will come and take us home to be with him and then we will inhabit our "mansion"; one that has been especially "built" for us.

Now back to 2 Corinthians 5:1–10. In verse 2 the imagery changes, and the concept of a building in which we live gives place to the idea of clothing which we are to put on. The heavenly dwelling that Paul longs to be clothed with is best understood as his resurrection body.[5] He is aware that the intermediate state, where we are without a body, is not the final destiny of humankind. He knows that he will one day receive a resurrection body—his heavenly dwelling—and spend eternity in the new heaven and new earth; and so he longs to be alive when Christ returns so that he can bypass the disembodied state and receive his resurrection body immediately. In verse 4 he tells us that while he is in "this tent," his earthly body, he groans because he would rather receive his resurrection body straight away than go through death and be unclothed in the

---

5. Beasley-Murray, *2 Corinthians*, 35. The author writes, "So close is this language to that which is used by Paul in 1 Corinthians 15:53f.it is difficult to believe that the same thought is not in mind here."

intermediate state. However, while that may be preferable, the thought of being at home with the Lord, even in a disembodied state, is so appealing that he would like to die so that he can experience this new level of intimacy (verse 8). For Paul it is a matter of "good, better, best." To be "in Christ" is good, to be with Christ in the intermediate state is better, but to have your resurrection body in the new heaven and new earth is the best.

When Paul says that he would prefer to be away from the physical body and be at home with the Lord (verse 8), we must remember that he was taken into heaven and shown things that he could not share with others. He knows what has been prepared for him and for us.

This passage also gives us a reason why we need to live with eternity in view. Christianity is not just a matter of me living a happier life, or having more money, or finding fulfillment here. We will leave this body one day and be at home with the Lord; therefore we should make it our goal to live in such a way that pleases him.

I think there is something within a child that wants to hear his father say, "Well done. I am proud of you." I remember seeing a TV musical talent show where one of the contestants had progressed through the various levels and had reached a certain stage, but his father would never recognize what he had achieved. After one performance the TV cameras showed this man phoning his father to tell him that he had progressed to the next round and then, with tears streaming down his face, emotionally pleaded with his father, "Please say that you are proud of me." One day every believer will stand before Christ to give an account of what he has done in this life. Paul urges us to live in such a way that when we face our heavenly Father we will hear him say, "Well done. I am proud of you." Refer to 2 Corinthians 5:9–10, "So we make it our goal to please him, whether we are at home in the body or away from it. For we must all appear before the judgment seat of Christ, that each one may receive what is due him for the things done while in the body, whether good or bad."

IS THE BELIEVER IN THE INTERMEDIATE STATE AWARE OF WHAT IS HAPPENING ON EARTH?

I have heard it taught that believers who are with God in heaven will be able to see everything that is happening on earth but will not be able to do anything about it. I do not believe this is true for being in the presence of God is a time of intimacy and joy. Imagine the anguish of a father in heaven if he could look down on earth and see his children rebelling against God by committing all types of evil, and not be able to do anything about it. That would be worse than being on earth; for there he could at least do something about the situation. Hebrews 12:1 tells us that "we are surrounded by such a great cloud of witnesses." We should not understand this verse, which refers back to the heroes of faith in chapter eleven, as saying that these people are spectators who are watching us, but rather they are inspiring examples for us to follow.

However, I do believe that God will give us selected glimpses of what is happening on earth that will cause us great joy. I have no verses from the Bible to support this, but I was talking to God one day and telling him that I wished my father was alive to see how he is using me in Africa, because I know that it would bring my father much joy. I felt that God said, "He does know."

THE FATE OF THE UNBELIEVER IN THE INTERMEDIATE STATE

Comments on Luke 16:19–31: the Rich Man and Lazarus

We have very little information concerning the fate of the unbeliever in the intermediate state. Paul says nothing about their state in his letters.[6] The main evidence comes from Jesus' teaching in Luke 16:19–31. When we try to understand this passage the first question we need to ask is, "Is this a true story or a parable to illustrate a central point?" Much of the argument for the former is based on the fact that Jesus gives a name to the poor man: "Lazarus." This is a powerful argument and one that we shouldn't dismiss lightly.

However, I believe this passage is best understood as a parable. Geldenhuys, who also maintains that this portion of Scripture is a parable, writes the following about verse 22, "These words prove that we should not regard the parable as a literal historical occurrence, for Abraham had died like other people and only his spirit is in the abode of bliss—not until after the resurrection at the second coming will his spirit and glorified body be united. So we cannot take in a literal sense the description given here of 'carried by the angels into Abraham's bosom.'"[7]

---

6. Ladd, *The Last Things*, 85.
7. Geldenhuys, *Commentary on the Gospel of Luke*, 428, fn6.

Furthermore, the name Lazarus, which is the Greek form of the Hebrew "God has helped," enables us to understand the meaning of the passage a little clearer. The reason that the poor man (Lazarus) went to Abraham's side is not because he was poor but because he relied on God and therefore "God helped him." The reason that the rich man went to hell is not because he was rich, but rather he saw himself as self-sufficient and therefore not needing God's help. It is a parable about a rich man who was self-centered, concerned only about himself and his luxurious lifestyle, and a person who relied on God, for "God has helped" him.

If it is a true story, and Lazarus simply happens to be the poor man's name, then it presents some problems, the foremost being that the teaching suggests that a person's destiny is determined by the amount of wealth he has: "But Abraham replied, 'Son, remember that in your lifetime you received your good things, while Lazarus received bad things, but now he is comforted here and you are in agony'" (verse 25). We know from Scripture that it is our faith in Christ that determines our eternal destiny and not the amount of money we may or may not have. However, if it is a parable, then the name "Lazarus" is crucial because it shows that the poor man didn't go to Abraham's bosom because he was poor, but because he relied on God when he was alive, and therefore God has helped him.

The parable shows that nothing changes after death regarding our standing with God; if we reject God before death then we will be rejected by God after death. If we turn to God for help prior to death then God will help us after death. It is our relationship with God in this life that determines our relationship to God in the afterlife. The Jews thought that wealth was a sign that a person was blessed by God, and hence was right with him, but this parable, and Jesus' response to the Rich Young Ruler in Luke 18:18–27, show that wealth doesn't automatically preclude one from the Kingdom of God, though it makes it difficult, since the rich are more likely to rely on their own self sufficiency than turn to God.

There are two main things we can discover from this passage about Lazarus and the Rich Man:

- There is no second chance after death, for there is a great gulf between the righteous and the ungodly.
- The eternal state for the righteous is pure bliss while the unbeliever only has torment to contemplate.

Where do the unrighteous go when they die? This parable said that the rich man went to "hades" but that doesn't fully answer the question. The Septuagint (the Greek translation of the Hebrew Old Testament) uses hades to translate the Hebrew "*Sheol*," which means the grave. The New Testament uses it in a similar way to the Hebrew in Acts 2:27,31, where the NIV translates it as "grave." In other passages, it seems to be synonymous with death and the two are linked together: "death and hades" (Rev. 1:18; 6:8). Other times "hades" seems to be more evil and even refers to hell. For example, in Matthew 16:18 the KJV translates it as "the gates of hell" and the NIV offers this as an alternate translation.

Interestingly, the translators of the NIV place this parable in hell for they translate verse 23 as, "In hell, where he was in torment, he looked up and saw Abraham far away, with Lazarus by his side." This translation has support from a number of sources. For example, Leon Morris writes, "In the New Testament, however, it [*hades*] is never used of the saved. Here it seems to be the equivalent to Gehenna, the place of punishment, for the rich man was *in torment*."[8] If this is right, and Jesus sets this parable (or true story) in hell, then this parable or story tells us nothing about the condition of the unrighteous in the intermediate state.[9]

Is the Unbeliever in Torment During the Intermediate State?

Another question we should ask is, "Do the unrighteous suffer intense torment from God while they are in the intermediate state?" I would say that the New Testament doesn't tell us directly, but there are a few things that we do know.

- John 3:36, "Whoever believes in the Son has eternal life, but whoever rejects the Son will not see life, for God's wrath remains on him." This tells us that God's wrath is on everyone who rejects Christ. This wrath continues after the unbeliever dies.
- Romans 2:5, "But because of your stubbornness and your unrepentant heart, you are storing up wrath against yourself for the day of God's wrath, when his righteous judgment will be revealed." While the unbeliever is under the wrath of God while he is alive,

---

8. Morris, *Luke*, 253. Tolbert writes, "*Hades* is used here only in the New Testament as a synonym for Gehenna (Tobert, , *Luke*, 132)."

9. Ladd concurs with this when he writes, ". . . it [the New Testament] sheds no light on the state of the unrighteous dead (Ladd, *The Last Things*, 39).

this is nothing compared with the wrath that he will experience on the day of judgment when he will be judged and thrown into the lake of fire. Note that this wrath doesn't descend on the unbeliever when he dies but only on the day of judgment. It seems to me that it would be unjust to punish someone before he or she has been judged and found guilty. Maybe this is why the translators of the NIV have translated the Greek "hades," in the parable of the Rich Man and Lazarus, as "hell" and see the parable as being set there.

- We do know that God, while he may not punish unbelievers upon physical death, is holding them for punishment: "The Lord knoweth how to deliver the godly out of temptations, and to reserve the unjust unto the day of judgment to be punished" (2 Peter 2:9 KJV). Refer also to the alternate translation of the NIV, "the Lord knows how to rescue godly men from trials and to hold the unrighteous for punishment until the day of judgment." These translations show that God is keeping the unrighteous until the day of judgment when they will be punished. I don't think the NIV is right when it has as its main option, "while continuing their punishment." I think the emphasis in the New Testament is that God's judgment will be revealed on the day of wrath; that is, the final judgment, and not at physical death. This "holding the unrighteous for punishment" is like the police charging a criminal and holding him in a cell while he awaits his trial before a judge.

- The unbeliever will probably endure some form of torture in the intermediate state but it may be self-induced. By this, I mean that he will realize that he is being held for judgment and that his life has not measured up to the standards of a holy God. He will realize that he has no hope as he awaits this fearful judgment. He may remember the times when he heard the gospel preached but laughed at it and now he is full of remorse that he didn't respond to the offer of salvation when it was given to him. He knows what awaits him and this must produce a sense of torment within him. Maybe, on the other hand, if he is being held for punishment and is surrounded by evil rather than good, he may also find himself tortured by his environment.

In summary, I believe that the unbeliever is kept by God for the day of judgment as a prisoner is held waiting the time of the trial. On that day they will be found guilty and thrown into the lake of fire; their punishment will commence on that date and not before. However, they may go through torment while in this intermediate state for they will be surrounded by evil and know that there is no second chance to get right with God. This realization that punishment is inevitable must produce some form of torture within them.

THE BIBLE DOESN'T TEACH ABOUT PURGATORY OR PRAYING FOR THE DEAD

In Roman Catholic teaching, purgatory is the place where the souls of believers go to be further purified from sin until they are ready to be admitted into heaven. Suffering in purgatory is seen as a good work that is offered to God as a substitute for the punishment that the soul should have endured because of the sins it committed while on earth. However, there is nothing in the New Testament to support this teaching, which seems to be based on 2 Maccabees in the Apocrypha—a selection of books that neither the Jews nor the Protestant church ever recognized as authoritative.

Paul, instead of talking about a period of suffering to purify his soul, talks about being immediately in the presence of God (Phil 1:23). These issues are important because they center on what a person must do in order to be saved; is it faith alone or good works? Romans 8:1 tells me that, "there is now no condemnation to those who are in Christ Jesus, because through Christ Jesus the law of the Spirit of life set me free from the law of sin and death." I do not have to suffer to pay for my sin, for Christ suffered in my place. Refer also to 1 Peter 3:18, "For Christ died for sins once for all, the righteous for the unrighteous, to bring you to God."

We see from the above that man's destiny is determined by his actions while he is alive on earth. If he is right with God, he goes immediately into the presence of his Lord, but if he has rejected God then he is separated from God. There is no second chance. Some have wanted to say that 1 Peter 3:19-20 points to another chance because Jesus preached to the spirits in prison. However, this is not so. While there are a number of interpretations of these difficult verses, we must note that it only applied to the people who lived at Noah's time, which is a minute number compared with all people who had previously lived. If it refers to a literal preaching to spirits in hell (and we have to ask ourselves why did he only preach to those who lived during the time Noah was building the ark?), then it was a proclamation of victory, for there is no mention of any invitation for salvation. (I think the most likely explanation for these verses is that they refer to the time when Noah was preaching to the unbelievers around him. In a way, Christ was preaching to them through Noah, but now they are spirits in hell because of their unbelief.)

We can say that there is no point praying for people who have already died, for their destiny has already been decided. We can, and at times should, thank God for the influence that godly people have had on our lives.

3

The Second Coming of Christ

INTRODUCTION

The term, "The Second Coming of Christ," is not found in the Bible, but it is a good way of describing this biblical truth. The closest we get to this phrase is found in Hebrews 9:28, "so Christ was sacrificed once to take away the sins of many people; and he will appear a second time, not to bear sin, but to bring salvation to those who are waiting for him." The first time Christ came was as a baby in order to initiate salvation, and the second time will be when he comes to take us to be with himself, and then, after a period of time, to introduce the new heaven and new earth. This will be the completion of our salvation.

The three main Greek words that the New Testament writers use to describe this event are: "parousia," "apokalypsis," and "epiphaneia." As we examine these words, and the context in which they are used, we get a better picture of the second coming and what it means.

- Parousia. This is the most common Greek word that is used to describe the return of Christ and means "coming," although there are some instances where it means "arrival" or "presence." Refer to 1 Thessalonians 4:15, "According to the Lord's own word, we tell you that we who are still alive, who are left till the coming of the Lord, will certainly not precede those who have fallen asleep."
- Apokalypsis means "revelation" or "revealed." Refer to 2 Thessalonians 1:6–7, "God is just: He will pay back trouble to those who trouble you and give relief to you who are troubled, and to us as well. This will happen when the Lord Jesus is revealed from heaven in blazing fire with his powerful angels."

- Epiphaneia can be translated as "manifestation" or "appearing." Refer to 2 Timothy 4:8, "Now there is in store for me the crown of righteousness, which the Lord, the righteous Judge, will award to me on that day—and not only to me, but also to all who have longed for his appearing."

BODILY AND VISIBLE RETURN

The New Testament tells us that we are to look forward to a sudden, personal, visible, bodily return of Christ to this earth.

- Acts 1:10–11. "They were looking intently up into the sky as he was going, when suddenly two men dressed in white stood beside them. 'Men of Galilee,' they said, 'why do you stand here looking into the sky? This same Jesus, who has been taken from you into heaven, will come back in the same way you have seen him go into heaven.'"
- 1 Thessalonians 4:16, "For the Lord himself will come down from heaven, with a loud command, with the voice of the archangel and with the trumpet call of God, and the dead in Christ will rise first."
- Revelation 1:7, "Look, he is coming with the clouds, and every eye will see him."

THE RETURN OF CHRIST IS A SINGLE EVENT

I believe that the New Testament teaches that the second coming of Christ will be one single, powerful, glorious event that will be visible to all.

There is a theological system called "dispensationalism" which divides the return of Christ into two events that are separated by seven years. The first phase is the rapture, when Christ secretly comes "for the saints" and takes the believers out of the world to be with him for seven years in heaven. At the end of this period he then returns "with his saints"; this is his return to set up his millennial rule and establish his earthly kingdom. This second phase of the second coming of Christ is referred to as the "revelation" (apokalypsis) and "appearing" (epiphaneia). Under this system the believer looks forward to the rapture, for this is when he will be caught up to be with Christ and escape the Great

Tribulation, which, dispensationalists teach, will take place on earth during this period.

While I was raised under this system of dispensationalism, I no longer believe it is what the Bible teaches. The New Testament writers look forward to the "revelation" (apokalypsis) of Christ as well as his "appearing" (epiphaneia) and his "coming" (parousia), as the following passages show. Furthermore, some of these verses raise a number of difficulties concerning the seven-year gap that is supposed to separate the parousia (commonly referred to as "the rapture" in dispensationalism) from the return of Christ.

- 1 John 2:28, "And now, dear children, continue in him, so that when he appears we may be confident and unashamed before him at his coming" (parousia).

- James 5:8, "You too, be patient and stand firm, because the Lord's coming (parousia) is near."

- 1 Corinthians 1:7, "Therefore you do not lack any spiritual gift as you eagerly wait for our Lord Jesus Christ to be revealed" (apokalypsis). Paul tells us that we are to eagerly look forward to the "apokalypisis" of Christ, but if this revealing occurs seven years after the rapture, during which time the saints have been enjoying the presence of God in heaven, why would we be looking forward to it? Surely, it is only the parousia that we would look forward to if the return of Christ is in two phases. Furthermore, we will not need spiritual gifts in heaven for that is when they will cease.

- 2 Thessalonians 1:6–7, "God is just: He will pay back trouble to those who trouble you and give relief to you who are troubled, and to us as well. This will happen when the Lord Jesus is revealed (apokalypsis) from heaven in blazing fire with his powerful angels." This passage tells us that the believer will finally receive relief from persecution when Christ is revealed (apokalypsis) from heaven. If the coming of Christ is a single event then this makes sense. However, if the "revelation of Christ" happens seven years after the "rapture," when the saints have been enjoying fellowship with God in heaven, then it seems contradictory, for the believer will not be experiencing persecution in heaven; no one will be troubling him there. Dispensationalism teaches that the believer will be free from persecution at the parousia; that is, when he is raptured with the rest of the saints. That is different from what Paul is saying in these verses from 2 Thessalonians.

- 1 Timothy 6:14, "I charge you to keep this command without spot or blame until the appearing (epiphaneia) of our Lord Jesus Christ." The epiphaneia of Christ occurs at the same time as the revelation of Christ and, according to dispensational teaching, comes after the believer has been in heaven for seven years with God. Yet Paul implies that the believer can sin up to the time of the appearing of Christ. If the second coming is one event then this doesn't present a problem, but if the coming of Christ is in two stages separated by seven years, when the believer has already been with God in heaven, then it does. Why would Paul tell Timothy to avoid sinning until the appearing of Christ if he has already been in heaven for seven years? You can't sin in heaven. The answer is simple: the second coming of Christ is one event and not two separated by seven years, or whatever period people want to suggest.

- Titus 2:12-13, "It teaches us to say 'No' to ungodliness and worldly passions, and to live self-controlled, upright, and godly lives in this present age, while we wait for the blessed hope—the glorious appearing (epiphaneia) of our great God and Savior, Jesus Christ." Why would the believer be waiting for the appearing of Christ, if he has already been in heaven for seven years? Again note that the believer has the ability to sin by giving in to ungodliness and worldly passions right up to the "appearing" of Christ. How can he sin if he is in heaven? If we see the coming of Christ as one event, and not two separated by seven years, then these verses in Titus make sense.

The "revelation," "appearing," and "coming" of Christ all refer to the one event, which we commonly refer to as "the second coming of Christ." There are no grounds to see it as two events separated by a period of time. Separating them by seven years and having the believer in heaven with God during that time only creates problems with what the Bible teaches.

COMMENTS ON DANIEL 9:24-27

I can hear my dispensational friends asking about Daniel 9:24-27 and the seventieth week. They interpret this to show that Christ's return is in two phases separated by a period of seven years. Let us look at that passage now.

> Seventy "sevens" are decreed for your people and your holy city to finish transgression, to put an end to sin, to atone for wickedness, to bring in everlasting righteousness, to seal up vision and prophecy and to anoint the most holy. 25 "Know and understand this: From the issuing of the decree to restore and rebuild Jerusalem until the Anointed One, the ruler, comes, there will be seven 'sevens,' and sixty-two 'sevens.' It will be rebuilt with streets and a trench, but in times of trouble. 26 After the sixty-two 'sevens,' the Anointed One will be cut off and will have nothing. The people of the ruler who will come will destroy the city and the sanctuary. The end will come like a flood: War will continue until the end, and desolations have been decreed. 27 He will confirm a covenant with many for one 'seven.' In the middle of the 'seven' he will put an end to sacrifice and offering. And on a wing of the temple he will set up an abomination that causes desolation, until the end that is decreed is poured out on him." (Dan 9:24–27)

By way of introduction let me say that it is best to understand "sevens" (NIV), or a "week" (KJV), as representing seven years; that is, one day equals one year. Therefore, sixty-nine weeks would equal 483 years. With this background let us now examine Daniel 9:24–27.

Verse 25 tells us that the Anointed One, the Messiah, will come sixty-nine weeks (seven weeks plus sixty-two) after the issuing of the decree to restore and rebuild Jerusalem. However, the question is, "When was this decree issued?" Many regard the letter that Artaxerxes gave to Ezra in Ezra 7:11 as being that decree, and I would agree with that. This event occurred during the seventh year of Artaxerxes' reign (Ezra 7:8); placing it in the year BC 458. If we add 483 years (69 times 7) to BC 458 we arrive at AD 25, the approximate time that Jesus started his public ministry. (Remember, Jesus was born somewhere between BC 4–6.) This is truly a remarkable prophecy!

Verse 26 reads, "After the sixty-two 'sevens,' the Anointed One will be cut off and will have nothing." It is best to see this as referring to the crucifixion of Jesus in approximately AD 29.

The point of departure between my dispensational friends and myself is the seventieth week as found in Daniel 9:27. Does this prophecy refer to events that occurred in the first century or something that is still in the future? I believe it relates to the former, and therefore everything in the vision that Daniel received was fulfilled by AD 70.

When we examine verse 24 we see six things that God was going to achieve through the life and death of Jesus, the Anointed One. All of this was to be accomplished by the end of the seventieth week.

- "To finish transgression, to put an end to sin, to atone for wickedness." This describes beautifully what Christ did on the cross. He was the "once for all sacrifice" that dealt with sin; animal sacrifices for sin were no longer required. He made atonement for sin and put an end to sin in that its power had been broken: "But now he has appeared once for all at the end of the ages to do away with sin by the sacrifice of himself" (Heb 9:26). This is why Jesus could say from the cross, "It is finished."

- "To bring in everlasting righteousness." Because of the death of Christ, we now have everlasting righteousness as a gift, something that we receive by faith.

- "To seal up vision and prophecy." Christ fulfilled all the prophecies of the Old Testament that spoke about the coming messiah. He brought the Old Covenant to an end and introduced the New: "By calling this covenant 'new,' he has made the first one obsolete; and what is obsolete and aging will soon disappear" (Heb 8:13).

- "To anoint the most holy." God anointed Jesus with the Holy Spirit before he began his public ministry.

I believe that all of Daniel 9:24–27, which refers to the entire seventy weeks, was fulfilled by Jesus in his first coming and during the years which immediately followed it. I believe that verse 26b, "The people of the ruler who will come will destroy the city and the sanctuary," describes the destruction of Jerusalem and its temple in AD 70 by Titus Vespasian, who later became emperor of Rome. I understand verse 27b, "And on a wing of the temple he will set up an abomination that causes desolation, until the end that is decreed is poured out on him," to have also been fulfilled in the events associated with the destruction of the temple in AD 70. (Refer to my discussion on Matthew 24:15 later in this chapter for a fuller discussion of the phrase, "the abomination that causes desolation.")

Dispensational teaching interprets verse 27 differently. They believe that the "prophetic clock" stopped after the sixty-ninth week (the first coming of Christ) and will not start again until the rapture, when Christ comes "for his saints." This event restarts the "prophetic clock," according to this teaching, and the seventieth week begins. During this "week" the Antichrist makes a covenant with Israel which will last seven years, but in the middle of it he breaks his covenant, disrupts the animal sacrifices in the rebuilt temple in Jerusalem, and launches a terrible persecution against the Jewish people. (Dispensational teaching assumes that the temple has been rebuilt in Jerusalem and that the sacrificial system has been reinstituted by this time.) At the end of the seventh year, Christ returns with his saints to destroy the antichrist and begin his millennial reign on earth.

Let me say that I have no objection to the idea that there is a large period of time between verse 26 and verse 27 if this is required by the context of the passage. Later on in this chapter I will discuss the concept of "prophetic foreshortening," where future events lose the perspective of time and often seem to merge together. However, I do not see any evidence in the Daniel passage that would support the idea that there is such a period of time between verses 26 and 27. I do not see any evidence to suggest that the events associated with verse 27 are still in the future. There is no explicit mention of the antichrist in verse 27, nor is there anything that suggests that it relates to the second coming of the Anointed One (Jesus).

I would maintain that everything associated with the sixty-ninth and seventieth weeks, as detailed in verse 24 and those that follow, was fulfilled by AD 70, and this includes the "abomination that causes desolation" as described in verse 27.

Some have suggested that Christ is the one who puts an end to sacrifice by his death on the cross. The book of Hebrews certainly teaches this (Heb 10:8–18). Furthermore, Christ ministered for three years after he began his public ministry and before he died; this would correspond with the time frame of "in the middle of the seven (years)," as mentioned in verse 27. On the other hand, was Titus the one who broke the covenant that Rome had established with the Jewish people when he invaded Jerusalem and destroyed the temple? The Jews had religio licita (legal sect) status in the Roman Empire that enabled them to continue their religion along with their various sacrifices, even though they were under Roman rule. When Titus destroyed the temple he certainly put an end to sacrifices and thereby broke the covenant that the Jews had previously enjoyed.

It is not my intent to give a full exegesis of this Daniel passage here, but instead to show that the messianic interpretation (the first coming of Christ) fits this prophecy far better than the eschatological one (the second coming of Christ). I do not see any valid reason for suggesting that Daniel teaches that the return of Christ will be in two stages separated by seven years.

WE DO NOT KNOW THE TIME BUT WE ARE TO BE READY

The New Testament teaches that we do not know exactly when Jesus will return though we should be ready when he does.

- Matthews 25:13, The Parable of the Ten Virgins, "Therefore keep watch, because you do not know the day or the hour."

- Mark 13:32–33, "No one knows about that day or hour, not even the angels in heaven, nor the Son, but only the Father. Be on guard! Be alert! You do not know when that time will come."

- Luke 12:39–40, "But understand this: If the owner of the house had known at what hour the thief was coming, he would not have let his house be broken into. You also must be ready, because the Son of Man will come at an hour when you do not expect him."

This should be sufficient warning against trying to predict the day when Christ will return, but unfortunately people still insist on doing it. The Jehovah's Witnesses have made many predictions concerning the specific date when Christ would return, but they have all proven to be wrong. In order to save face, they claim that Christ did return on October 1, 1914, as they predicted, but that he came in an invisible way. However, this denies the biblical teaching that Christ's return will be bodily and visible.

Even Bible-believing Christians have fallen into this trap. I remember a few years ago, when all the planets in the solar system were going to momentarily line up, this was seen as the time when Christ would return. My wife responded to people who were promoting this teaching by saying that we can't predict the time, because the Bible tells us that we do not know the hour when Christ will return. Their reply was, "We may not know the hour, but we know the day." This is to misunderstand the meaning of the Greek word "hora," which is translated "hour" in this verse. It is best to understand "hora" here in the more general sense: the general time when something will take place and not necessarily a sixty minute period of time.[1]

These verses are crucial for they emphasize the need to be ready for the return of Christ. We are to live our life as if Christ could return today. I heard a preacher tell how John Wesley, the founder of the Methodist church, was asked one evening what he would do tomorrow if he knew Christ was coming back at the end of that day. John Wesley was reported to have opened his diary and then listed the things that he had already planned to do; he was ready for Christ's return. Some people would change their plans for they know that there are things that God has called them to do that they have not done. There are people they should forgive, sins they should repent of, or people to whom they should speak about the Lord. If we are ready for Christ's return then we will not be embarrassed when he comes.

For me, this is the main reason to study eschatology. It reminds us of the eternal perspective and that this life is not our permanent and final destiny. It reminds us to live with eternity in view and to create priorities that take this into account. We study eschatology not to satisfy our intellectual curiosity, but to live in a way that pleases God, knowing that there is more to life than what we are currently experiencing.

CHRIST'S RETURN CAN HAPPEN ANY TIME

It is hard to read the New Testament without getting the impression that the early church lived with the expectation that Christ could return at any time. Consider the following verses:

- Philippians 3:19b–21, "Their mind is on earthly things. But our citizenship is in heaven. And we eagerly await a Savior from there, the Lord Jesus Christ, who, by the power that enables him to bring everything under his control, will transform our lowly bodies so that they will be like his glorious body."

- Titus 2:12–13, "It teaches us to say 'No' to ungodliness and worldly passions, and to live self-controlled, upright and godly lives in this

---

1. Grudem, *Systematic Theology*, 1093–94.

present age, while we wait for the blessed hope—the glorious appearing of our great God and Savior, Jesus Christ."

- James 5:7–9, "Be patient, then, brothers, until the Lord's coming. See how the farmer waits for the land to yield its valuable crop and how patient he is for the autumn and spring rains. You too, be patient and stand firm, because the Lord's coming is near. Don't grumble against each other, brothers, or you will be judged. The Judge is standing at the door!"

- 1 Peter 4:7, "The end of all things is near. Therefore be clear minded and self-controlled so that you can pray."

- Revelation 22:20, "He who testifies to these things says, 'Yes, I am coming soon.' Amen. Come, Lord Jesus."

I believe that the second coming of Christ is imminent. By that I mean that Christ could come at any time and that we should be ready for his return. This doesn't mean that he will definitely come this year, or even in my lifetime, but he could come tonight or next week. The imminent return of Christ doesn't mean that I should not develop long-term plans—on the contrary—but if he does come tonight I should not be embarrassed because I have not done what I should have done.

We must not think that the New Testament writers were wrong because Christ did not return in their lifetime. God has a different perspective on time, as 2 Peter 3:8–9 shows, "But do not forget this one thing, dear friends: With the Lord a day is like a thousand years, and a thousand years are like a day. The Lord is not slow in keeping his promise, as some understand slowness. He is patient with you, not wanting anyone to perish, but everyone to come to repentance." Not only is a thousand years on earth as a day to God, but a day to us may be as a thousand years to him.

Where the Bible talks prophetically about events happening "soon" we need to understand that prophets saw things as two-dimensional (height and width) rather than three-dimensional (height, width, and depth). This is sometimes referred to as "prophetic foreshortening." Let me give a practical example of this. When one watches a cricket match on TV, the cameras are, of necessity, a long way away from what is happening in the middle of the oval. As a consequence, when a fast bowler ("pitcher" for baseball fans) is operating, the wicketkeeper ("catcher" for baseball fans) seems to stand relatively close to the wicket ("home plate" for baseball fans). I remember very clearly going to watch my first international cricket match at the Sydney Cricket Ground. The match had just started and I was watching it on television. I said to my wife Carol, "I would love to go and watch a game one day." She suggested that I go, and so off I went. The game was in progress when I arrived, and I went to take my seat, which was to the side of the wicket. This meant that instead of looking down the wicket, as the TV cameras did, I was looking across the wicket. I clearly remember being puzzled, for the fast bowler was walking back to his mark to start his run, and the wicket keeper and slips fieldsmen were standing almost halfway towards the boundary fence. I remember saying to myself, "When are they going to move up closer to the wicket so that they are in their normal position." They didn't move closer because they were in the right position. The large telescopic lens on the TV cameras distorted the idea of depth so that the wicketkeeper seemed to be a lot closer to the wicket than he actually was. Prophecy is like that. As the prophet "looks down the telescopic lens of time," the near and distant futures blend together so that everything looks as if it is going to happen "soon."

CHRIST'S RETURN WILL COME LIKE A "THIEF IN THE NIGHT" WHEN EVERYTHING SEEMS TO BE NORMAL

The idea that we do not know when Christ will return, and that it could be at any time, is confirmed by the biblical teaching that his return will come like a "thief in the night." This suggests that Jesus will come when we least expect it. He will return when everything seems to be going on as it always has and people are saying, "peace and safety" (1Thess 5:3). Consider the following verses:

- Matthew 24:42-44, "Therefore keep watch, because you do not know on what day your Lord will come. But understand this: If the owner of the house had known at what time of night the thief was coming, he would have kept watch and would not have let his house be broken into. So you also must be ready, because the Son of Man will come at an hour when you do not expect him." Jesus himself uses the analogy of a thief in the night to describe his coming and tells us that it will happen when we do not expect it.

- Matthew 24:37-39, "As it was in the days of Noah, so it will be at the coming of the Son of Man. For in the days before the flood, people were eating and drinking, marrying and giving in marriage, up to the day Noah entered the ark; and they knew nothing about what would happen until the flood came and took them all away. That is how it will be at the coming of the Son of Man." In these verses Jesus clearly states that things will be "normal" immediately prior to his return. In the days of Noah people were going about their business as they always had, "people were eating and drinking, marrying and giving in marriage." There were no signs of any impending judgment, just a "silly old man" building an ark. That is how the return of Christ will be. Things will be going on as they always have and there will be no signs to say anything is different; just some "silly old preachers" calling people to repent. Then, like a thief in the night when we least expect it, Christ will return.

- Matthew 25:1–13. The Parable of the Wise and Foolish Virgins. Both the wise and foolish virgins (believers and unbelievers) were asleep when the bridegroom came. There was nothing to suggest that he was about to come and so they became drowsy and fell asleep. His return was like a "thief in the night" when everything seemed to be going along as it always had.

- 1 Thessalonians 5:1–3, "Now, brothers, about times and dates we do not need to write to you, for you know very well that the day of the Lord will come like a thief in the night. While people are saying, 'Peace and safety,' destruction will come on them suddenly, as labor pains on a pregnant woman, and they will not escape." This is almost identical teaching to that given by Jesus in the above verses. The coming of the Lord will occur when people are saying, "Peace and safety," rather than when the situation is so bad that people, believer and unbeliever alike, are saying that the end of the world could be upon us.

- Revelation 16:15, "Behold, I come like a thief! Blessed is he who stays awake and keeps his clothes with him, so that he may not go naked and be shamefully exposed." This verse tells us to stay awake; that is, to be living in such a way that we will not be embarrassed when Jesus returns. "Being awake" doesn't mean that we will be able to tell when the thief will come, but that we will be ready whenever that may be. I believe this is what Paul means in

1 Thessalonians 5:4 when he writes, "But you, brothers, are not in darkness so that this day should surprise you like a thief." If we are certain that Christ will return, and if we are living a holy life, then we will not be surprised when he comes. I do not believe there will be signs to tell us that he is about to come, but we should be ready to welcome him when he does. I believe that Christ can come at any time.

- Peter also uses the same imagery in 2 Peter 3:10a, "But the day of the Lord will come like a thief."

The Cold War between the USA and the Soviet Union was at its peak when I was a teenager, and I remember the fear that gripped people during that time. The Cuban Missile Crisis was a worry for many people, and I clearly remember the night when the US warships were sent to intercept the Russian ships carrying the missiles. I remember standing in the living room of my parent's home in Sydney, Australia, wondering if World War III, with the resultant destruction of the world, had commenced on the other side of the globe. There was great expectation that these were the "last days" and that Christ was about to return.

However, I remember my father saying that it probably would not happen then because Scripture tells us that Christ will come back when people are saying, "peace and safety." People, including those who attended church and those who didn't, were not saying "peace and safety" in those days; rather, they were quite fearful and worried. I am not suggesting that we will see "peace and safety," and hence universal peace, in every area of the world immediately prior to Christ's return, but that the world will continue on as it always has. The world as a whole will be experiencing "peace and safety," while some pockets will be immersed in war and conflict as it always has.

I understand the above verses to be crucial in regard to our understanding of the return of Christ. They seem to be straight forward—they are neither apocalyptic nor metaphorical in form—he will return like a thief in the night when things seem to be going on as normal. We will not have any warning that he is coming and there will be no signs that tell us that he is about to come or that his coming is getting near. The concept of a "thief in the night" precludes signs that tell us that the coming of "the thief" is close; thieves do not give you any hint as to when they may break into your house.

ARE THERE SIGNS THAT WILL TELL US THAT CHRIST IS ABOUT TO RETURN?

Let us now examine the signs of Christ's coming, if there are any, concentrating on Mark 13, Luke 21, and Matthew 24.

Introduction to the Signs

Are there signs that can tell us that the return of Christ is about to take place?

Before we discuss this topic allow me to make some general comments.

- If there are signs that have yet to be fulfilled, then Christ cannot come at any time.
- If Christ can come at any moment then all the signs must have been already fulfilled.
- If Christ is going to come like a thief in the night when we least expect it, then the signs that are yet to happen, if there are any, can not be very dramatic otherwise we would know that Christ is about to come.

I do not think that there are any signs that have to be fulfilled.

When preachers talk about the coming of Christ they often look at the world around them and note how there are "wars and rumors of wars," "earthquakes in various places," "false prophets," and interpret these events as signs that the return of Christ is near. However, I do not believe that this is how we are to understand these verses. I do not believe that they are referring to "signs" which tell us that the return of Christ is getting close.

Let us examine the two groups of verses that are most commonly used in this regard—those that refer to the "last days," and the teaching of Jesus from Matthew 24 and parallel passages—and see what they teach.

The Last Days

There are a number of verses in the New Testament that mention the "last days." For example, 2 Timothy 3:1–5a, "But mark this: There will be terrible times in the last days. People will be lovers of themselves, lovers of money, boastful, proud, abusive, disobedient to their parents, ungrateful, unholy, without love, unforgiving, slanderous, without self-control, brutal, not lovers of the good, treacherous, rash, conceited, lovers of pleasure rather than lovers of God—having a form of godliness but denying its power." However, the term "the last days" doesn't refer to the days immediately prior to Christ's return but to the whole period from his first coming up to his second. For example, in Acts 2:17 Peter quotes from Joel to show that the "last days" were present at Pentecost. In Hebrews 1:1–2a we read that the "last days" began with the ministry of Jesus: "In the past God spoke to our forefathers through the prophets at many times and in various ways, but in these last days he has spoken to us by his Son." The same idea is present in 1 Peter 1:20, "He was chosen before the creation of the world, but was revealed in these last times for your sake." Therefore, we should not understand passages that speak of "the last days" as referring solely to the time immediately prior to our Lord's return. Behavior that characterizes the "last days," such as that listed in 2 Timothy 3:1–5, is not a sign showing that Christ is about to return; rather it tells us that man will always be like this until Christ comes back.

Background to Matthew 24, Mark 13, and Luke 21

As I mentioned earlier, popular preaching that surrounds the second coming often talks about "signs" such as: "wars and rumors of wars," "famines and earthquakes in various places," "preaching of the gospel to all nations," and "false prophets who show signs and wonders." All these "signs" come from the parallel passages of Matthew 24, Mark 13, and Luke 21, so let us examine them in more detail.

Let us start with Mark's account of this incident. It commences with Jesus' comment in verse 2 that the Temple will be so completely destroyed that not even one stone will be left upon another. Later on, as they were sitting opposite the temple on the Mount of Olives, some of the disciples asked Jesus when destruction of the temple would take place, and what would be the signs it was about to happen. "Tell us, when will these things happen? And what will be the sign that they are all about to be fulfilled?" (Mark 13:4). Luke gives us the same thought using almost identical wording: "'Teacher,' they asked, 'when will these things happen? And what will be the sign that they are about to take place?'" (Luke 21:7) One of the principles of biblical interpretation is that the context determines the meaning. The context of Mark and Luke is clearly the destruction of the Temple; that is the question Jesus was asked and that is the question that he sets out to answer. If the only record we had of this teaching by Jesus came from Mark and Luke, then we would see this passage, with its reference to "wars and rumors of wars," as referring solely to the destruction of the Temple in AD 70 by the Roman army, and not referring in anyway to the second coming of Christ.

However, Matthew gives us a slightly different account by modifying the question that the disciples asked: "As Jesus was sitting on the Mount of Olives, the disciples came to him privately. 'Tell us,' they said, 'when will this happen, and what will be the sign of your coming and of the end of the age?'" (Matt 24:3). Now the question is not only about the destruction of the Temple but also about the coming of Christ and the end of the age. We don't know why Matthew has the question in a slightly different form but maybe the disciples thought that the destruction of the temple was so unthinkable that, if it were to happen, it had to mean the return of Christ and the end of the age. Maybe Matthew knew that Jesus went beyond simply discussing the destruction of the Temple and combined it with his own coming and the end of the age.

I believe that the best way to understand this passage, often known as the "Olivet Discourse," is to see it as referring primarily to the destruction of Jerusalem in AD 70, when God did come in judgment on his people, but also containing elements that look forward to the second coming of Christ. Therefore, the signs in Matthew 24:5-22, and parallel passages, were fulfilled in AD 70 when Jerusalem was destroyed. However, not everything in this "Olivet Discourse" relates to God's judgment on the Jewish nation in AD 70 but some verses, especially Matthew 24:30-31, talk about the second coming of Christ.

Comments on Matthew 24:5-22

With the above in mind, let us examine the signs as found in Matthew 24:5-22.

- Verse 5, "For many will come in my name, claiming, 'I am the Christ,' and will deceive many."
- Verse 6, "You will hear of wars and rumors of wars, but see to it that you are not alarmed. Such things must happen, but the end is still to come."

- Verse 7, "Nation will rise against nation, and kingdom against kingdom. There will be famines and earthquakes in various places."
- Verse 9–10, "Then you will be handed over to be persecuted and put to death, and you will be hated by all nations because of me. At that time many will turn away from the faith and will betray and hate each other."
- Verse 11, ". . . and many false prophets will appear and deceive many people."
- Verse 14, "And this gospel of the kingdom will be preached in the whole world as a testimony to all nations, and then the end will come."
- Verses 15–16, "So when you see standing in the holy place 'the abomination that causes desolation,' spoken of through the prophet Daniel—let the reader understand—then let those who are in Judea flee to the mountains."
- Verses 21–22, "For then there will be great distress, unequaled from the beginning of the world until now—and never to be equaled again. If those days had not been cut short, no one would survive, but for the sake of the elect those days will be shortened."

When we examine Josephus and other first and second-century historians, we note that all of these signs were fulfilled in the fall of Jerusalem in AD 70. The fourth-century church historian Eusebius, notes that the Christians fled to a city in Perea called Pella before the destruction of Jerusalem, and so were saved from the devastation.[2] It appears that the early church understood these verses, and the signs that they mention, as referring to the destruction of the Temple in AD 70. History shows that Jesus' comment in verse 2 that "not one stone here will be left on another" was fulfilled literally, for people even pried apart the stones to collect the gold leaf that melted from the roof when the temple was set on fire.

With this in mind, let us look at these verses in more detail. Verse 5 says, "For many will come in my name, claiming, 'I am the Christ,' and will deceive many" and verse 11 says, "many false prophets will appear

---

2. Eusebius, *Ecclesiastical History* III.V.3, quoted by Lane, *The Gospel according to Mark*, 468.

and deceive many people." Josephus notes that during the government of Felix (AD 53–60) "the country was full of robbers, magicians, false prophets, false Messiahs and impostors, who deluded the people with promises of great events."[3] He also tells us of an Egyptian false prophet who gathered a following of about 30,000 and led them to the Mount of Olives, preparing to launch an attack on Jerusalem, but the Romans under Felix overcame them, killing and imprisoning many.[4] Jesus' predictions in verses 5 and 11 were certainly fulfilled by the events that culminated in the destruction of Jerusalem in AD 70.

Concerning verse 6, "hearing of wars and rumors of wars," it is possible that Jesus was referring to the period of civil war and insurrection that followed the death of the Roman emperor Nero in AD 68. It would certainly fit.

Verse 7 says, "Nation will rise against nation, and kingdom against kingdom. There will be famines and earthquakes in various places." This fits with what we know of the period leading up to the destruction of Jerusalem. Geldenhuys writes, "In AD 61 there had been a severe earthquake in Phrygia, which had done vast damage . . . in 63 an eruption of Vesuvius had laid half of Pompeii in ruins; there had been famines in the reigns both of Claudius and Nero, the Jewish rebellion against Rome, and the war which led to the capture and destruction of Jerusalem, had begun or was to begin in AD 66."[5] The Roman historian Tacitus also gives us a similar picture of that period.[6]

Verse 14 is "And this gospel of the kingdom will be preached in the whole world as a testimony to all nations, and then the end will come." If we were to take this in a scientific and literal way we know that there are still some tribes that have not heard the gospel message, and therefore this verse was not fulfilled in the first century. However, we can see this statement of Jesus fulfilled by AD 70, for Paul writes in Colossians 1:5–6, 23 that this gospel is bearing fruit all over the world and that it has been proclaimed to every creature under heaven. If we are to take this verse literally then believers in, say, the nineteenth century would have known that the return of Christ was a long way off and certainly not imminent.

3. Sproul, *The Last Days according to Jesus*, 34.

4. Josephus, *War* 2.261–63, quoted by Morris, *The Gospel According to Matthew*, 606; cf. Acts 21:38.

5. Geldenhuys, *Commentary on the Gospel of Luke*, 531, fn10.

6. Sproul, *The Last Days according to Jesus*, 122–23.

If we are to understand that the early church expected Christ to return at any time then we cannot interpret this verse (Matt 24:14) literally, rather we are to interpret it in light of what Paul says in the above verses from Colossians.

Verses 15–16, "The abomination that causes desolation, spoken of through the prophet Daniel," referred initially to the act of desecration of the temple in Jerusalem in BC 168 when Antiochus Epiphanes erected a pagan altar to Zeus over the sacred altar, sacrificing a pig and making Judaism a capital offence (Dan 11:31). Jesus' use of this term suggests that he sees a second fulfillment of this prophecy in the future, and when people see it they should flee Jerusalem. However, what is the "abomination that causes desolation"? We know that it refers in part to the invading Roman armies with their pagan standards, for Luke substitutes the phrase, "the abomination that causes desolation" (Matt 24:15; Mark 13:14) with, "when you see Jerusalem being surrounded by armies, you will know that its desolation is near" (Luke 21:20). We understand this to be the case by looking at the three Gospels and comparing what immediately precedes Jesus' command to flee Judea. In Matthew and Mark it is the "abomination that causes desolation" while in Luke it is the Roman armies; hence the conclusion that the "abomination that causes desolation" is, in part, the invading Roman armies.

However, it seems that the phrase "the abomination that causes desolation" also refers to a person, for Mark uses a masculine participle to modify a neuter noun. We know from history that the Temple was desecrated in ways other than by those of the Roman armies, for Josephus tells us about criminals who were able to roam freely around the temple, including the Holy of Holies. This desecration seems to have culminated in the appointment of the clown Phanni as high priest. Lane gives us a summary of what happened by quoting from Josephus.

> During this period the Zealots moved into and occupied the Temple area (*War* IV.iii.7), allowed persons who had committed crimes to roam about freely in the Holy of Holies (*War* IV.iii.10), and perpetuated murder within the Temple itself (*War* IV.v.4). These acts of sacrilege were climaxed in the winter of 67–68 by the farcical investiture of the clown Phanni as high priest (*War* IV.iii.6–8). It is in response to this specific action that the retired high priest Ananus, with tears, lamented: "It would have been far better for me to have died before I had seen the house of God laden with such abominations and its unapproachable and hal-

lowed places crowded with the feet of murderers" (*War* IV.iii.10). Jewish Christians who had met in the porches of the Temple from the earliest days would have found this spectacle no less offensive. It seems probable that they recognized in Phanni "the appalling sacrilege usurping a position which is not his," consigning the Temple to destruction. In response to Jesus' warning they fled to Pella.[7]

Maybe it was the combination of the Roman armies surrounding the city and the sacrilege of Phanni that made the Christians realize that the prophecy of Jesus was about to be fulfilled. Geldenhuys writes the following about verse 21, "When the first signs appeared that Jerusalem was going to be surrounded by the Roman forces practically all the Christians fled from the city and its environs across the Jordan to the Trans-Jordanian town of Pella (the modern Kherbit-al-Fakil), where they remained until after the destruction of Jerusalem."[8] The signs given by Jesus in this Olivet Discourse were so accurate that when the time came, the Christians had no doubt that the signs were being fulfilled and fled Jerusalem as instructed by Jesus. There is no doubt in my mind that "the abomination that causes desolation" found its fulfillment in the events that immediately preceded the destruction of Jerusalem in AD 70.

Josephus, the Jewish historian, also saw the fulfillment of the Daniel prophecy concerning the "abomination that causes desolation" in the events of AD 66–70. He wrote, "in the same manner Daniel also wrote about the empire of the Romans and that Jerusalem would be taken and the Temple laid waste."[9]

Verse 21 states, "For then there will be great distress, unequaled from the beginning of the world until now—and never to be equaled again." Josephus describes the horrors of the siege of Jerusalem and its destruction in his written history. He relates how during the famine that was caused by the siege, a woman took her baby whom had been sucking at her breast and killed it. She then roasted her own child, ate half of its body, and offered the rest to bystanders. The onlookers expressed utter contempt for her actions and left the scene in a spirit of trembling. Josephus then describes the Romans burning the temple and placing Jerusalem under the ban, "While the holy house was on fire, everything

---

7. Lane, *Mark*, 469.
8. Geldenhuys, *Luke*, 527–28.
9. Josephus, *Antiquities* X.xi.7, quoted from Lane, *Mark*, 468.

was plundered that came to hand, and ten thousand of those that were caught were slain; nor was there a commiseration of any age, or any reverence of gravity; but children and old men, and profane persons, and priests, were all slain in the same manner; so that this war went round all sorts of men, and brought them to destruction . . . "[10] It is said that not a single Jew was left alive in the city; they were either slaughtered or taken away as prisoners of war.[11] We can see that Jesus' words, "For then there will be great distress, unequaled from the beginning of the world until now," were literally fulfilled in AD 70.

The second part of verse 21 is interesting, "and never to be equaled again." Many Bible-believing scholars interpret verse 21 as referring to the destruction of Jerusalem in AD 70 but also pointing forward to a more devastating period of persecution immediately prior to the return of Christ. I fail to see this, for verse 21 clearly says that the distress associated with the destruction of Jerusalem in AD 70 will never be equaled again.

Verse 22, "If those days had not been cut short, no one would survive, but for the sake of the elect those days will be shortened," is referring to Israel as a whole. We know from Josephus that no one survived in Jerusalem, but fortunately the Romans didn't continue on with a systematic destruction of the whole nation. Had the days not been cut short, and had the Romans continued on to destroy the rest of Israel, it is likely no one would have survived. It is interesting that this further destruction of Israel was prevented for the "sake of the elect": the believers. It is a constant theme throughout the Old Testament that God withholds judgment on a nation because of the righteous. In the case of Sodom and Gomorrah, it would have been averted had there been ten righteous people.

It is also interesting that Titus, the Roman general, saw the hand of God in the destruction of Jerusalem. He is reported to have said, "God, indeed, has been with us in the war, God it was who brought down the Jews from these strongholds; for what power have human hands or engines against these towers?"[12]

Luke 21:25 refers to signs in the heavens: "There will be signs in the sun, moon and stars. On the earth, nations will be in anguish and perplexity at the roaring and tossing of the sea." This was also fulfilled

---

10. Sproul, *Last Days according to Jesus*, 121.
11. Geldenhuys, *Luke*, 528.
12. Morris, *Matthew*, 606, fn 36.

in the period associated with the destruction of the temple in AD 70. Both Josephus and the Roman historian Tacitus mention signs in the sky during this time. Consider the following from Josephus,

> Thus there was a star resembling a sword, which stood over the city, and a comet, that continued a whole year. Thus also, before the Jews' rebellion, and before those commotions which preceded the war, when the people were come in great crowds to the feast of unleavened bread, on the eight day of the month Xanthicus [Nisan], and at the ninth hour of the night, so great a light shone round the altar and the holy house, that it appeared to be bright day time; which light lasted for half an hour. This light seemed to be a good sign to the unskillful, but was so interpreted by the sacred scribes, as to portend those events that followed immediately upon it.[13]

Josephus also mentioned other occurrences in the heavens,

> Besides these, a few days after that feast, on the one-and-twentieth day of the month Artemisius [Jyar], a certain prodigious and incredible phenomenon appeared; I suppose the account of it would seem to be fable, were it not related by those that saw it, and were not the events that followed it of so considerable nature as to deserve such signals; for, before sun-setting, chariots and troops of soldiers in their armor were seen running about among the clouds, and surrounding of cities. Moreover at the feast which we call Pentecost, as the priests were going by night into the inner [court of the] temple, as their custom was, to perform their sacred ministrations, they said that, in the first place, they felt a quaking, and heard a great voice, and after that they heard a sound as of a great multitude, saying, Let us remove hence.".[14]

Tacitus wrote of this period, "Besides the manifold misfortunes that befell mankind, there were prodigies in the sky and on the earth, warnings given by thunderbolts, and prophecies of the future, both joyful and gloomy, uncertain and clear. For never was it more fully proved by awful disasters of the Roman people or by indubitable signs that the gods care not for our safety, but for our punishment."[15]

---

13. Sproul, *Last Days according to Jesus*, 122.
14. Ibid., 124.
15. Ibid., 123.

In summary, it seems to me that all the signs mentioned in Matthew 24:1–22 and parallel passages were fulfilled in the destruction of Jerusalem in AD 70.

Which Verses Refer to the Second Coming of Christ in the Olivet Discourse?

The difficulty with the Olivet Discourse is knowing when Jesus switches from talking about the destruction of Jerusalem in AD 70 and when he starts discussing his second coming. I am sure that the teaching up to Matthew 24:22 refers to the destruction of Jerusalem in AD 70, and that Matthew 24:30–31 refers to the second coming. The verses between these two blocks are a little uncertain, but I believe that they are referring to the return of Christ.

Let us examine Matthew 24:30–31 first. It is hard to read these verses and not think that Jesus is referring to his visible, bodily return to earth: "At that time the sign of the Son of Man will appear in the sky, and all the nations of the earth will mourn. They will see the Son of Man coming on the clouds of the sky, with power and great glory. And he will send his angels with a loud trumpet call, and they will gather his elect from the four winds, from one end of the heavens to the other." They bear a striking parallel to the angel's words in Acts 1:9–11, "After he said this, he was taken up before their very eyes, and a cloud hid him from their sight. They were looking intently up into the sky as he was going, when suddenly two men dressed in white stood beside them. 'Men of Galilee,' they said, 'why do you stand here looking into the sky? This same Jesus, who has been taken from you into heaven, will come back in the same way you have seen him go into heaven.'" Jesus will return in the same way as he went: visibly in bodily form. Matthew 24:30–31 refers to this visible, bodily return of Christ and not to an invisible return to bring judgment on the Jewish nation through the Roman army, as some have taught.

The concept of the loud trumpet call accompanying the second coming of Christ, along with the gathering of the elect, as mentioned in Matthew 24:31, is also found in 1 Thessalonians 4:16–17: "For the Lord himself will come down from heaven, with a loud command, with the voice of the archangel and with the trumpet call of God, and the dead in Christ will rise first. After that, we who are still alive and are left will be caught up together with them in the clouds to meet the Lord in the air.

And so we will be with the Lord forever." This clearly refers to the second coming of Christ when the righteous dead will be resurrected; further confirming that, Matthew 24:30–31 also refers to the same event.

How do we understand the intervening verses, Matthew 24:23–28? I believe that they describe the manner of Christ's return. Before proceeding any further, let me note that verse 23 takes us forward through the centuries to the events associated with Christ's return even though this long period of time is not overtly mentioned. This should not surprise us because we noted earlier that "prophetic foreshortening" makes distant events merge with those in the immediate future, so that one seems to follow on from the other. The idea that verse 23 refers to the events surrounding our Lord's return is reinforced by verse 30. Note how both verses begin with "At that time," suggesting that both are talking about the same period of time. Since verse 30 is referring to the visible return of Christ, we can conclude that verse 23 is also dealing with the same event: his bodily return.

The first thing that Jesus tells us in Matthew 24:23–28 is that many false Christs will appear and that we are not to be deceived by this. The second thing he teaches is to not pay attention to anyone who says that he has returned to earth and only appeared to a small handful of witnesses in some obscure village in China or in the mountains of central USA. Do not believe these reports. This is not the way Christ is going to appear. When he comes it will be as obvious as lightning flashing across the sky, or as clear as vultures circling around a carcass. We will all know when he returns; it will be spectacular and visible to everyone. "So if anyone tells you, 'There he is, out in the desert,' do not go out; or, 'Here he is, in the inner rooms,' do not believe it" (verse 26). Refer also to Jesus' words in verses 27–28, "For as lightning that comes from the east is visible even in the west, so will be the coming of the Son of Man. Wherever there is a carcass, there the vultures will gather."

Verse 29 then goes on to tell us that one aspect of Christ's coming will be to bring judgment upon the world. "Immediately after the distress of those days 'the sun will be darkened, and the moon will not give its light; the stars will fall from the sky, and the heavenly bodies will be shaken.'" We should not interpret this verse in a literal or scientific way, but see it as a metaphor that describes Christ returning in judgment. This is confirmed by the fact that Jesus quoted from Isaiah 13:10. This verse in Isaiah, which describes God's judgment on the Babylonians, is metaphorical rather than a scientific description of what God was going to do. Therefore, we should understand Matthew 24:29 in the same way as we interpret Isaiah 13:10. Can you imagine the turmoil and horror that would occur if verse 29 is literally true, as something that will happen in a period that leads up to the second coming? If the sun was darkened and the moon didn't give light, and if the stars fell from the sky and the heavenly bodies were shaken, I imagine that there would be a fair amount of panic. This is contradictory to what Jesus taught in the latter part of the Olivet Discourse when he described his coming in terms of a "thief in the night," when everything will continue as it always has (Matt 24:36–25:13).

Matthew 24:24 is an interesting verse, "For false Christs and false prophets will appear and perform great signs and miracles to deceive even the elect—if that were possible." We will discuss the nature of the Antichrist, or man of lawlessness as Paul calls him in 2 Thessalonians, later in Chapter 4, but if he is someone who propagates false doctrine as I suggest, then this verse in Matthew could well be referring to him.

Let us now look at Matthew 24:32–33, "Now learn this lesson from the fig tree: As soon as its twigs get tender and its leaves come out, you know that summer is near. Even so, when you see all these things, you know that it is near, right at the door." What does this refer to? Is it the destruction of Jerusalem in AD 70 or the second coming of Christ? I believe it is the former and that Jesus returns to answer the main thrust of the question, "When will the temple be destroyed so that 'not one stone here will be left on another'"? I have already mentioned that we know from history that the early Christians understood the invasion of the Roman army in AD 70 as being the fulfillment of Matthew 24:5–22 and fled Jerusalem. Jesus' comment in verse 43, that his visible return would be like a thief in the night when we are not expecting him, suggests that he is not referring to his second coming in these verses (Matt 24:32–33), but to the events associated with AD 70.

Matthew 24:34 is an intriguing verse: "I tell you the truth, this generation will certainly not pass away until all these things have happened." How are we to understand this verse if part of Jesus' teaching refers to something that is still in the future? One solution is to say that it only applies to what Jesus said about the destruction of Jerusalem but doesn't include the few verses about his second coming. There is some support for this view, because I believe that the preceding two verses refer to the destruction of the temple rather than the second coming. If that is the case, then verse 34 would be an extension of what Jesus said in verses 32–33, and apply to the events of AD 70.

However, I prefer the interpretation that says that the Greek word can be translated "race," and this is how we should understand it. Jesus is saying that although Jerusalem will be destroyed, the Jewish race will not vanish but will still exist when he returns. The fact that the Jews were scattered throughout the world for almost two thousand years and were able to keep their identity, even though they didn't have a homeland, is nothing short of miraculous. Maybe verse 34 is meant to be pastoral in tone, to encourage the Jews that God has not abandoned them and that they are still his covenant people. God may have brought punishment upon them because of their rejection of Jesus as their messiah, but he has not rejected them (Luke 19:41–44).

Verse 36 is another reminder that no one knows the hour or the day when Christ will return: "No one knows about that day or hour, not even the angels in heaven, nor the Son, but only the Father."

We discussed verses 37 to 39 earlier, but the point Jesus seems to be making is that we are to be ready even though we don't know when he will return. "For in the days before the flood, people were eating and drinking, marrying and giving in marriage, up to the day Noah entered the ark; and they knew nothing about what would happen until the flood came and took them all away. That is how it will be at the coming of the Son of Man." There will be no signs for everything will be going on as it always has. People will be absorbed with the activities of everyday life and will know nothing about his return until it is too late. Therefore be ready!

Verses 40–41 take place when Christ returns. "Two men will be in the field; one will be taken and the other left. Two women will be grinding with a hand mill; one will be taken and the other left." The believers who are alive when Christ comes back will be caught up to meet him in the clouds while the unbelievers will be left behind. From this position in the clouds, all believers, including those who had previously died, will then come down to earth with their resurrection bodies, and Christ will begin his millennial reign. Sadly, the unbelievers will be left as they had previously been.

The remainder of the chapter is an exhortation to live a life worthy of our calling as believers; Christ will come on a day when we do not expect him and at an hour that we are not aware of (verse 50). I remember an incident in Africa that highlighted the importance of this. I was in the middle of explaining this passage when all of a sudden my interpreter had an insight into what I was teaching and interrupted me to say, "I see now that if there are no signs associated with Christ's return then it is more important that I live a godly life now so that I am ready. If there were signs then I would have time to change my life before Christ came."

FURTHER DISCUSSION ON THE "ANY MOMENT" RETURN OF CHRIST AND THE SIGNS OF HIS COMING

I mentioned earlier in this chapter that I believe that Christ could return at any time and that we need to be ready for him. However, not all scholars agree with me. They have said that there are significant and dramatic signs that must first take place before Christ returns, and therefore, since these events are still in the future, he can't come back at any moment. These signs are usually associated with Matthew 24:5–22. For example, they maintain that these verses are a "foreshadow" or "type"[16] of what will happen in the future, and so they are expecting, among other things, a time of great distress which will be even worse than that associated with the destruction of the Temple in AD 70. As a result of this, they say that Christ can't return at any time.

I have problems with this view. For example, it seems to diminish the expectancy of Christ's coming that we find in the New Testament, and it seems to minimize the urgency of being ready for his return. Time and again we see warnings in Scripture to be awake and ready for the Lord to come back, for he will come like a thief in the night when we do not expect him. Refer to Luke 12:40: "You also must be ready, because the Son of Man will come at an hour when you do not expect him." If Christ's return is a long way off, because there are certain signs that are far off into future, then why the urgency to be ready for his return? Jesus said in Luke 12:40 that he will come when we do not expect him. It is hard to see how this can be true if there are obvious signs that must first take place. This interpretation doesn't seem to do justice to Jesus' teaching that we are to be awake and ready. He has told us that he is

---

16. A "type" is a person, thing, or event that serves as an illustration of another thing. For example, the Passover lamb in Exodus 12 is a type of Christ because it illustrates the significance of his death on the cross (1 Cor 5:7).

coming when we do not expect him. The fact of Christ's coming is not unexpected; it is only the time of his return that is unexpected.

Other scholars have put forward differing views on this issue and they have varying degrees of merit. One view that I particularly like when applied to the man of lawlessness, the Antichrist, says that it is unlikely that the signs have been fulfilled but it is possible that they have.[17]

With the above in mind, what do I think is the most viable? I believe that the signs mentioned in the Olivet Discourse have already been fulfilled and that Christ could return at any time. I don't believe that they are a "type" of things which must occur some time in the future immediately prior to our Lord's coming. However, in regard to the Antichrist, the man of lawlessness, I do believe that the above view—it is unlikely but possible that he has already been revealed—is the best. This means that if he is already in our midst, which is possible, then Christ could return at any moment to destroy him. (Refer to chapter 4 for further discussion on this topic.)

SUMMARY ON SIGNS

I believe that all the "signs" mentioned in Matthew 24:1–22 and parallel passages have been fulfilled in the destruction of Jerusalem in AD 70 and that Christ could therefore return at any moment, like a "thief in the night" when everything seems to be going along normally. Therefore, we are to live our lives with eternal values in mind rather than being sidetracked by self-centered pursuits. Being ready for Christ's return means that we will not have to make any last minute changes on how we live in order to escape embarrassment when he appears.

If the first part of Jesus' teaching (Matt 24:1–22) was fulfilled in minute detail, even to the point where the stones were pried apart for the gold so that "not one stone was left on top of another," we can be assured that the second part of his teaching —namely, his visible bodily return—will also come to pass exactly as he foretold it.

---

17. Grudem, *Systematic Theology*, 1101. I do not believe that this argument is valid for the others signs, since I believe that they were fulfilled in the first century, but I do think it is a plausible argument in regard to the coming of the Antichrist.

OVERVIEW OF EVENTS THAT OCCUR AT THE RETURN OF CHRIST

The following is a summary of events that take place at the return of Christ:

- The Antichrist (or man of lawlessness) is destroyed.
- Believers who have died will return from heaven with Christ. Their bodies will be resurrected and transformed so that they receive their resurrection bodies while they are in the clouds.
- An instant later the believers who are still alive will be caught up to be with the Lord in the air and be transformed so that they receive their resurrection bodies.
- Both groups of believers will then continue to earth with Christ.
- Christ begins his physical reign on earth during the millennium.

4

The Great Tribulation and the Antichrist

THE GREAT TRIBULATION

Introduction

It is common in Bible-believing circles for people to refer to the great tribulation and ask the question whether Christians will be rescued from it or have to go through it. Dispensationalists maintain that the church will be raptured before the great tribulation and that the latter will be inflicted on the Jews who are still on the earth. (Remember, this view separates the coming of Christ, the parousia, and the revelation, or appearing of Christ, by seven years.) Other Bible-believing scholars maintain that the church will go through the tribulation and that Christ will return at the end of it to destroy the antichrist. I have one major problem with all of this in that I can't see a great tribulation, as described by these theological systems, clearly taught in the Bible.

Let us examine some of the reasons that godly Bible scholars give to support this concept of a "great tribulation," that either immediately precedes the coming of Christ or immediately follows it. Larkin, in *Dispensational Truth*,[1] finds support for the tribulation in Matthew 24:9–22 and Revelation 6:1—19:21 in the New Testament and Jeremiah 30:4–7, Daniel 12:1, and other passages from the Old. From this he concludes that the church will not go through the tribulation, for the church will have been taken out of the way since it has already been raptured, and that this fierce persecution, known as the great tribulation, will be

---

1. Larkin, *Dispensational Truth*, 133

directed against the Jews who are on the earth. In response to this let me say the following:

- First, I firmly believe that the New Testament doesn't teach that the return of Christ will occur in two stages that are separated by seven years. Therefore this sequence of events—the church being in heaven for a period of time while the Jews are still on the earth—is not possible.

- Second, I believe that Matthew 24:9–22 refers to the "tribulation" that accompanied the destruction of the Temple in AD 70 and not to some "great tribulation" associated with the return of Christ in the future. I will elaborate on this later.

- Concerning Revelation 6, we need to note that the dispensational view that Larkin advocates teaches that the parousia of Christ, the rapture, occurs in Revelation 4:1,[2] and that the chapters that follow talk about the seven-year period between the two phases of Christ's return. Apart from the fact that the second coming of Christ is one event, and not two separated by seven years, I have difficulty seeing how Revelation 4:1 refers to the coming of Christ. This verse talks about the apostle John being taken up into heaven in his vision. It seems almost impossible to see this verse as referring to the rapture of the entire church. There is nothing in Revelation that would give us any grounds to base this on. Therefore, I cannot see Revelation 6 as referring to something that will happen after the return of Christ but to a period of persecution that was about to descend on the early church. (There is more about this passage later.)

Other Bible-believing scholars see "the abomination that causes desolation, spoken of through the prophet Daniel" (Matt 24:15), as referring initially to the destruction of Jerusalem in AD 70, but also to the end times. Concerning this verse in Matthew, Ladd writes, "it refers also to the overthrow of Jerusalem by the Roman armies in 70 A.D. who desecrated the temple by bringing into its precincts the hated pagan standards. Beyond that it refers to the eschatological antichrist who will arise in the end time, of whom both Antiochus and Rome were fore-

---

2. I have read that some dispensational scholars are now advocating that the rapture occurs between the end of Revelation 3 and the beginning of chapter 4 and that the rapture is assumed. Arguing from silence is a very dangerous exercise.

shadowings. That he 'stands in the holy place' means that he demands the worship of men."[3] However, let me ask the question, "Why do the events of AD 70 foreshadow what is going to happen at the end?" Surely one would expect something more definite than a "foreshadow" if this was going to happen. Surely we should expect a clear statement in this regard and not implications?

Another reason why I do not think that the events associated with Matthew 24, especially verses 21 and 22, are a type of the eschatological antichrist (the Final Antichrist) is that they describe people who use totally different methods to achieve their goals. As we have previously noted, the Romans unleashed such physical destruction on Jerusalem that not one single Jew was left alive in the city; they were either slaughtered or taken away as prisoners of war. I can hear some readers saying that this is exactly what the man of lawlessness will do and this is why the events of AD 70 are a foreshadow that point towards the man of lawlessness, except the latter will be even more evil. Paul's teaching in 2 Thessalonians 2 is usually put forward to support this view. But when we examine 2 Thessalonians we find a totally different picture. What we find is someone who is able to perform counterfeit miracles, signs, and wonders, and, as a result of that, he deceives people (2 Thess 2:9–10a). The reason he can deceive them is "because they refused to love the truth and so be saved" (2 Thess 2:10b). This is not a picture of a man who unleashes fierce physical persecution to achieve his goals, but one who uses more subtle means and deceives people. Therefore, I believe that events associated with the destruction of the temple in AD 70 are not a type of what is going to happen immediately prior to our Lord's return.

When we look at the remainder of the Olivet Discourse, and especially Matthew 24:36 to 25:13, it is difficult to see Jesus teaching that there will be a time of great tribulation immediately prior to his return. I can't see that it will be a time "when the rule of law will collapse, when political order will be swept away and be unable any longer to restrain the principle of lawlessness,"[4] as some suggest. In Matthew 24:37–39, Jesus says the following about his return, "As it was in the days of Noah, so it will be at the coming of the Son of Man. For in the days before the

---

3. Ladd, *The Last Things*, 63

4. Ladd, *The Last Things*, 69. While I disagree with Ladd on this point, I do want to mention that I have found his books to be very informative and helpful over the years. Much of my theology has been molded by what he has written.

flood, people were eating and drinking, marrying and giving in marriage, up to the day Noah entered the ark; and they knew nothing about what would happen until the flood came and took them all away. That is how it will be at the coming of the Son of Man." There was no sign of the collapse of law, for the conditions, even though they were evil, continued as they had for years. I believe that this is the point that Jesus is trying to make. He doesn't talk about a "collapse of law" but rather refers to "people eating and drinking, marrying and giving in marriage." This paints a picture of normality, people enjoying themselves, life going on as it always has; it was not one of intense distress. In fact, "they knew nothing about what would happen until the flood came and took them away" (verse 39). Why? Because there were no signs that anything was substantially different to what they had always known.

People are more likely to turn to God when some calamity strikes but Jesus seems to be warning us that he will come like a thief in the night when everything seems to be going along as it always has. This is why we have to be ready at all times; we will not get any warning that the thief is about to break in.

The parable of the Wise and Foolish Virgins in Matthew 25:1–13 seems to reinforce this idea. Everything seemed to be normal; in fact, it was so "normal" that they all went to sleep. There is no sign here of a great tribulation immediately prior to the bridegroom's return. There was no warning and no signs that told the wise virgins that he was about to come; instead, he came like a "thief in the night" when he was not expected.

In 1 Thessalonians 5:1–3 Paul seems to be saying the same as Jesus, "Now, brothers, about times and dates we do not need to write to you, for you know very well that the day of the Lord will come like a thief in the night. While people are saying, 'Peace and safety,' destruction will come on them suddenly, as labor pains on a pregnant woman, and they will not escape." These words seem to rule out the idea that the time immediately prior to Christ's return will be accompanied by the collapse of the rule of law.

However, we must not conclude that Christians will be safe from persecution at the time immediately preceding Christ's second coming. Persecution is something that Jesus has warned his followers to expect; it started with the early church and it will continue until he comes back. Believers have certainly not been exempt from it in the twentieth century. Lewis A. Drummond writes, "In the 1990s alone, the martyrdom of some 290,000 Christians a year was recorded."[5] Another report that I have read put it over 300,000 a year. Whichever way we look at it, this is a lot of people killed each year simply because they claim to be followers of Jesus. This persecution has occurred in the Soviet Union, Uganda, China, Islamic nations, and elsewhere. When we look at the persecution around the world we note that it has been isolated, rather than a universal, organized program under the leadership of one person. I believe that persecution of the church will continue as it has from the beginning but there will not be a systematic "great tribulation" immediately prior to Christ's return. The observer will not be able to say, "The thief is about to come because of a sudden increase in the harassment of believers." Refer also to Matthew 24:21, "For then there will be great distress, unequaled from the beginning of the world until now—and never to be equaled again." The last phrase, the context of which refers to AD 70, seems to rule out a final great tribulation that is worse in intensity than anything we have previously seen; nothing will be more intense than the events surrounding the destruction of Jerusalem.

Let us now examine the passages where the term "great tribulation" is mentioned and try to discover their meaning. Depending on the version of the English Bible that one uses, there can be three references to this term. They are:

- Revelation 7:14 (NIV), "And he said, 'These are they who have come out of the great tribulation; they have washed their robes and made them white in the blood of the Lamb.'" The KJV, RSV, and NASB also use the phrase "great tribulation."

- Matthew 24:21 (NIV), "For then there will be great distress, unequaled from the beginning of the world until now—and never to be equaled again." The KJV, RSV, and NASB translate the Greek as "great tribulation" rather than "great distress."

- Revelation 2:22 (NIV), "So I will cast her on a bed of suffering, and I will make those who commit adultery with her suffer intensely, unless they repent of her ways." The KJV, RSV, and NASB translate the Greek as "great tribulation" rather than "suffer intensely."

---

5. Drummond, *The Evangelist*, 92.

Let us examine these passages one at a time.

- Revelation 7:14. One's understanding of this verse is determined by one's view of Revelation. I see the book as having been written to encourage first-century believers to stand firm in the face of persecution and not to think that God has lost control and that evil is about to triumph. The book of Revelation shows us that history is under the control of God, and that he will destroy the beast—which is first-century Rome and any other government that sets itself up against God—and bring his victory to pass. In Revelation 3:10, the church at Philadelphia in the first century was given this promise, "Since you have kept my command to endure patiently, I will also keep you from the hour of trial that is going to come upon the whole world to test those who live on the earth." This "hour of trial that was coming upon the whole world" had to happen during the lifetime of the believers who belonged to the first-century church at Philadelphia, otherwise the promise was meaningless. I believe this is the great tribulation that is spoken of in Revelation 7:14; it happened in the first century, or early second century at the latest. Revelation 7:14 is a source of encouragement to those in the first century who were about to be tested by this "trial that was coming upon the whole earth."

- Matthew 24:21. As I have mentioned a number of times, I believe the great distress mentioned in this verse relates to the horrific events that surrounded the destruction of the Temple in AD 70. I see no evidence to say that they are a type of a great tribulation that will happen at the end. Just because some versions of the Bible use the phrase "great tribulation" we must not jump to the conclusion that they are referring to a time immediately prior to our Lord's return.

- Revelation 2:22. This refers to a prophetess called Jezebel who belonged to the first century church at Thyatira, and who was misleading others into sexual immorality and eating food sacrificed to idols. Because of this, Christ was going to cause those who committed adultery with her to suffer intensely (or go through great tribulation) unless they repented. This reference to a great tribulation refers to an event in Thyatira in the first century and not to something that would immediately precede Christ's return.

I conclude that every reference in the New Testament to a great tribulation refers to events that occurred around the first century and not to a time that immediately precedes our Lord's second coming.

Finally, the other problem with the teaching of a universal great tribulation immediately preceding the return of Christ is that it seems to rule out the idea that Christ could return at any time. If there is going to be such a time of universal tribulation, which is associated with the appearance of the final antichrist who causes the rule of law to collapse, then Christ can't return while the world scene, as a whole, is normal and people are saying "peace and safety." This seems to remove the urgency to be watching for Christ's return because he could not come like a thief in the night if there are obvious signs that must take place first.

THE ANTICHRIST

The Antichrist in the Book of Daniel

It is common among Bible-believing scholars to say that the idea of Antichrist first appears in the Bible in the book of Daniel, although he is not referred to by that name. It is generally understood that Antiochus IV Ephiphanes, the king of the Syrian Seleucids who ruled Israel at that time (175–164 BC), was the forerunner or "type" of the Antichrist. Daniel 11 talks about the events associated with Antiochus Ephiphanes, including his attempt to destroy the Jewish religion and replace it with the religion of Greece. He ordered that all copies of the Old Testament be destroyed, he had a pig sacrificed on the great altar in the temple at Jerusalem, and he rededicated the temple itself to the pagan Greek god, Zeus Olympius. This happened in 168 BC and is described in Daniel 11:31, "His armed forces will rise up to desecrate the temple fortress and will abolish the daily sacrifice. Then they will set up the abomination that causes desolation."

What makes people think that Daniel 11 goes beyond the events of BC 168 and refers to the final antichrist is what is written in Daniel 11:36–37, "The king will do as he pleases. He will exalt and magnify himself above every god and will say unheard-of things against the God of gods. He will be successful until the time of wrath is completed, for what has been determined must take place. He will show no regard for the gods of his fathers or for the one desired by women, nor will he regard any god, but will exalt himself above them all." This goes beyond anything that Antiochus Ephiphanes did, and hence the feeling is that Daniel saw something beyond the Old Testament period and actually had an insight into the last days before the coming of Christ. The character of this antichrist figure is one who takes all divine character to himself and rewards those who worship him. Because of this, he is anti-God, which is also antichrist.

Antichrist in Matthew 24 and Parallel Passages

Many Bible-believing scholars see Matthew 24:15–16 as referring to the final antichrist, but I do not agree with that. In these verses Jesus makes reference to Daniel and the abomination that causes desolation: "So when you see standing in the holy place 'the abomination that causes desolation,' spoken of through the prophet Daniel—let the reader understand—then let those who are in Judea flee to the mountains." We have discussed these verses previously in chapter 3 but we can summarize this passage as referring to the invasion of Jerusalem by the Roman army under Titus and the events associated with it. Luke 21:20 equates this "desolation" with the Roman army. However, it seems that the "desolation that causes abomination" was a little wider than that and included the farcical investiture of the clown Phanni as high Priest. It is probable that Christians at the time saw in Phanni "the appalling sacrilege usurping a position which is not his," and knew that the Temple was doomed to destruction. Whatever the events that led up to this, they were so clear that the early Christians saw them as being the fulfillment of Jesus' prophecy in Matthew 24 and fled the city. I do not see a reference to the antichrist in these verses.

Paul tells us in 2 Thessalonians 2:9–10 that the man of lawlessness, the antichrist, will perform all kinds of counterfeit miracles, signs, and wonders, and he will deceive those who are perishing. This seems to be describing someone or something totally different to that mentioned in Matthew 24:15–16. The man of lawlessness sets out to deceive people while the Roman army used brute force. I don't believe that these passages in Matthew and 2 Thessalonians are referring to the same person. I conclude that Matthew does not describe the antichrist.

Antichrists in 1 John

In 1 John 2:18 we read, "Dear children, this is the last hour; and as you have heard that the antichrist is coming, even now many antichrists have come. This is how we know it is the last hour." This verse suggests that there will be a person called the Antichrist, however, says John, many antichrists have come, and I assume, will continue to come, until the final antichrist appears on the world scene. In fact, these early antichrists had originally been part of the Christian church (1 John 2:19).

First John 2:22 and 1 John 4:1–3 shed more light on the nature of these antichrists and the Antichrist; they are false teachers who deny that Jesus is from God. The immediate reference in 1 John is to the early Gnostics who taught that the divine Christ came upon the human Jesus at his baptism and left him at the cross, so that it was only the man Jesus who died. I have heard many a preacher say that Hitler was a forerunner of the antichrist because he set out to eradicate the Jewish people. Hitler may or may not be a type of the final antichrist, but that doesn't fit the teaching in 1 John. Here the antichrist is more a promoter of false doctrine and philosophy than someone who uses violence to achieve his goal.

It has been suggested that the philosophy of humanism, or even the New Age movement, could be the Antichrist or a forerunner of him because it deifies man. For example, Williams, when discussing the man of sin/lawlessness, who I believe to be the Antichrist[6], writes,

> As we noted above, Paul speaks of the man of sin as one "who opposes and exalts himself against every so-called God or object of worship." This sounds similar to secular humanism, which opposes every trace of religion and puts man and his self-fulfillment as the only legitimate concern. Thus, without saying so, secular humanism deifies man. Humanist man, accordingly, to use Paul's further words, is one "proclaiming himself to be God" . . . The New Age movement goes the further step of specifically identifying man with God. Whereas secular humanism declares there is no God, New Age thinking quite bluntly speaks of man as one with God and urges all people to realize their true identity . . . When this happens—and it is occurring in various shapes and forms throughout the New Age movement—surely we are not far removed from the man of sin who proclaims himself to be God.[7]

---

6. Refer to Morris, "The Antichrist," 40. "Paul does not use the term 'antichrist', but the 'man of sin' of whom he writes in 2 Thes.ii.3.ff clearly refers to the same being."

7. Williams, *Renewal Theology*, vol, 3, 338–9.

Comments on 2 Thessalonians 2:1–12

Background

This passage gives us a description of the man of lawlessness, whom we believe is also the antichrist. Second Thessalonians 2:4 describes him: "He will oppose and will exalt himself over everything that is called God or is worshiped, so that he sets himself up in God's temple, proclaiming himself to be God." Since Christ is fully God, the description of "antichrist" is an apt one for this man of lawlessness. The background to this final antichrist is as follows. Paul had told the Thessalonians in his first letter that when Christ returned they would be caught up into the air to meet him in the clouds and be with the Lord forever. But the Thessalonians had previously received a letter, or something like that, which had supposedly come from Paul, to say that the day of the Lord—that is, his return—had already come. One can imagine the alarm that the Thessalonians felt because this would have meant that they had been rejected by God, since they were still as they had always been.

Paul tells them that the return of Christ will not happen until "the rebellion" occurs and the man of lawlessness is revealed (verse 3). However, there is someone or something stopping the man of lawlessness from being revealed at the moment. Paul then reminds the Thessalonians that he had told them this when he was previously with them, and that they knew exactly what he was saying: "Don't you remember that when I was with you I used to tell you these things? And now you know what is holding him back, so that he may be revealed at the proper time" (Verses 5–6). The problem for us is that the Thessalonians knew what was holding the man of lawlessness back, and it was so obvious to them that Paul didn't have to state it. However, we do not know what it was and can only take guesses as to what it might have been. William Barclay calls this, "undoubtedly one of the most difficult passages in the whole New Testament; and it is so because it is using terms and thinking which were perfectly familiar to those to whom Paul was speaking but which are utterly strange to us. To those who read and heard it for the first time, it required no explanation at all; but to us, who have not their local knowledge, it is obscure."[8]

---

8. Barclay, *The Letters to the Philippians, Colossians, and Thessalonians*, 245 quoted in Hobbs, *Commentary on 1-2 Thessalonians*, 289.

The KJV has "man of sin" rather than "man of lawlessness." There are discrepancies in the Greek manuscripts, but the better manuscripts seem to favor "man of lawlessness."[9] However, there is no real difference between the two, for sin is lawlessness (1 John 3:4).

Appearance of the Antichrist and the Rebellion

Second Thessalonians 2:3 reads, "Don't let anyone deceive you in any way, for that day will not come until the rebellion occurs and the man of lawlessness is revealed, the man doomed to destruction." It seems that Paul envisages a surge in rebellion against God just prior to our Lord's return. It is as though Satan throws everything he can against God and his church in one last desperate effort. This rebellion does not mean that the church will decline because of a great falling away from the faith, as some teach. History shows that the church often grows as a result of persecution, if persecution is the result of the rebellion.

Unfortunately the KJV has incorrectly translated the Greek word *apostasia* as "falling away" and this, along with other passages, has led to the teaching that there will be widespread apostasy immediately prior to our Lord's return. Concerning this word, Morris writes, "In classical Greek the word '*apostasia*' denoted a political or military rebellion; but in the Greek Old Testament we find it used of rebellion against God (e.g. Jos.xxii.22), and this becomes the accepted Biblical usage."[10] We must not understand this verse as referring to apostasy. I was taught during my early years that the church would decline and almost disappear in the "last days," but when all seemed lost, Christ would return and take us all to heaven. This incorrect theology is based on a faulty translation of this verse and other passages.

The antichrist will be the person who will lead this rebellion. He is not Satan, for Paul draws a distinction between the two in verse 9, but he will be Satan's instrument to lead this final attack against God and his people. He will also have the power of Satan, even the ability to perform counterfeit miracles: "The coming of the lawless one will be in accordance with the work of Satan displayed in all kinds of counterfeit miracles, signs and wonders, and in every sort of evil that deceives those who are perishing" (2 Thess 2:9–10a).

---

9. Morris, *The Epistles of Paul to the Thessalonians*, 126.
10. Ibid.

THE MAN OF LAWLESSNESS IS BEING HELD BACK AT THE MOMENT

Paul told the Thessalonians that there was someone or something that was holding back the appearance of the antichrist: "And now you know what is holding him back, so that he may be revealed at the proper time. For the secret power of lawlessness is already at work; but the one who now holds it back will continue to do so till he is taken out of the way. And then the lawless one will be revealed, whom the Lord Jesus will overthrow with the breath of his mouth and destroy by the splendor of his coming" (2 Thess 2:6–8). Paul is saying that it was impossible for the antichrist to have been revealed when he wrote the letter for there was a power that was keeping him back. This power is referred to in verse 6 as a neuter noun—an impersonal thing ("what" is holding him back)—but in verse 7 Paul uses the masculine particle of the same verb (the "one" who holds it back), meaning that he is also a person. The combination of masculine and neuter nouns leads many commentators to see a reference to the Roman Empire, which might be referred to as a "thing" (the Empire) or a "person" (the Emperor who personified the Empire).[11]

As we mentioned above, it was clear to the Thessalonians what the restraining power was, but we have no idea. However, the fact that Paul talks about the secret power of lawlessness in verse 7, plus the role of the Roman Empire at that time, has led some people to see the restraining power as referring to the principle of law and government. The Roman Empire provided peace and protection for its citizens and this helped the church to expand quickly, but there came a time when later emperors turned against the church, and hence that restraining power of law and order was removed and the church was fiercely persecuted. Some scholars suggest that the "restraining power" is the rule of law and order, that one day in the future will be withdrawn and the man of lawlessness will be revealed and persecute the church. For example, Ladd writes, "Paul sees a day when the rule of law will collapse, when political order will be swept away and be unable to restrain the principle of lawlessness."[12]

This idea of "law and order collapsing" presents great difficulties for me. In 1 Thessalonians 5:2–3 Paul tells us that the "day of the Lord will come like a thief in the night. While people are saying, 'Peace and safety,' destruction will come on them suddenly, as labor pains on a pregnant

---

11. Ibid., 129.
12. Ladd, *The Last Things*, 68–69.

woman, and they will not escape." This hardly seems to describe a situation where the principle of law and order has broken down—in fact it seems to be the opposite.

I was taught in my early years that the power holding back the appearance of the antichrist is the Holy Spirit and that he will be removed from the earth when the church is raptured to heaven for seven years. The great tribulation will then occur during this time. However, we have already noted that the return of Christ will be a single event, rather than one having two phases separated by seven years, and this rules out the possibility of this sequence of events. Furthermore, there doesn't seem to be any textual reason to say that the one who holds back the man of lawlessness is the Holy Spirit.

Antichrist Destroyed by the Coming of Christ

The antichrist will be destroyed by Christ when Christ returns: "And then the lawless one will be revealed, whom the Lord Jesus will overthrow with the breath of his mouth and destroy by the splendor of his coming" (2 Thess 2:8). This is not a prolonged struggle, or even a physical battle, but an instantaneous victory and destruction of the antichrist.

I believe that Revelation 19:17–21 describes the return of Christ and his victory over the antichrist and his evil colleagues. This is also the battle of Armageddon which was announced back in Revelation 16:12–16. We know that this battle is associated with the return of Christ because Jesus says, "I come like a thief," words which are used elsewhere to describe his return. John doesn't mention the antichrist by name in Revelation, but the events that he describes are those that relate to the man of lawlessness whom we believe is the antichrist. Revelation 19:19 describes how the enemies of God are ready for battle but John never describes the battle—he simply tells us that the beast and false prophet were thrown into the lake of burning sulfur (verse 20). The reason for this is that there is no battle. There is no fighting because Christ defeats them and the rest of the armies, "with the sword that came out of the mouth of the rider of the horse" (verse 21). The victory is instantaneous. This is exactly how Paul describes it in 2 Thessalonians 2:8; Christ defeats the man of lawlessness by the breath of his mouth and the splendor of his coming. I love the last concept, for the nature of the risen Christ is so powerful that just his presence destroys the forces of evil.

I do not believe that we are meant to understand the battle of Armageddon as a physical battle. Revelation is written in an apocalyptic style, and these vivid symbols describe a spiritual battle, but, as with everything spiritual, it will have physical consequences.

Pulling It All Together

Anyone who attempts to write on matters relating to eschatology needs to do so with a great deal of humility. There are certain truths that Bible-believing scholars can agree on—such as the absolute certainty of the personal return of Christ—but some other issues are not as clear. With this in mind, allow me to summarize what I think is the best interpretation of the Bible in regard to the antichrist/man of lawlessness and the great tribulation.

There are a number of views that I can't see as being correct.

- First, dispensational teaching sees the antichrist as appearing after the rapture of the church and before the return of Christ to set up his millennial reign on earth. I can't see any teaching in the New Testament that suggests that the parousia and revelation/appearing of Christ are two separate events separated by a period of time.

- The other view that I don't see in Scripture is that Christ will return after the "great tribulation," during which time the man of lawlessness will reign, resulting in a total collapse of law. I have difficulty in seeing a "great tribulation" immediately prior to our Lord's return. This doesn't seem compatible with Jesus' and Paul's teaching that Christ's return will be like a thief in the night when everything is continuing along as normal. While this doesn't rule out persecution of believers, it does imply that there will be no breakdown of law and order immediately prior to our Lord's return.

- Another reason why I don't think that the events in Matthew 24:21–22 are a type of a final great tribulation is that it doesn't match the teaching of Paul in 2 Thessalonians 2:9–10. In Matthew 24, the Romans used intense physical force to achieve their goals but the man of lawlessness seems to use more subtle means so that he deceives people.

- Finally I can't see that Matthew 24:21–22 supports the concept of "the great tribulation" and that it occurs immediately prior to our Lord's return. While the KJV translates verse 21 as "For then shall be great tribulation," we must not assume that it refers to the time prior to our Lord's return simply because it uses the phrase, "great tribulation." This verse refers to the distress that accompanied the destruction of the Temple in AD 70. The verse goes on to say that this time of great distress "will be unequalled from the beginning of the world until now—and never to be equaled again." The latter phrase seems to rule out any possibility that the events of AD 70 are a type of what will occur prior to the return of Christ; they will not be equaled again.

What does appear to be feasible?

- John in his first epistle tells us that the antichrist is associated with false teaching that sets itself up against Christ The only time the word "antichrist" is used in the Bible is in John's epistles. Here it clearly relates to false teaching and deceiving people: "Many deceivers, who do not acknowledge Jesus Christ as coming in the flesh, have gone out into the world. Any such person is the deceiver and the antichrist" (2 John 7).

- I was raised on a steady diet of teaching that maintained that the antichrist was an evil dictator, so it is difficult for me to completely dismiss this idea. If we knew who or what was holding the man of lawlessness back in 2 Thessalonians 2:6–7, we would have a better understanding of who or what he was. However, 2 Thessalonians 2:9 tells us that the man of lawlessness will be able to perform counterfeit miracles, signs, and wonders. This suggests that he is going to be more than an evil tyrant who simply uses force to get people to worship him—if he is that at all. As far as I know, neither Antiochus IV Ephiphanes (BC 175-64), nor "the abomination that causes desolation" as described in Matthew 24:15 and fulfilled in AD 70, or Hitler, or Stalin, or Henry Kissinger, or any other modern person who people have thought to be the antichrist, ever performed counterfeit miracles, signs, and wonders.

- Paul tells us in 2 Thessalonians 2:10 that the man of lawlessness, "deceives those who are perishing," but they perish "because they refused to love the truth and so be saved." Here again the emphasis

The Great Tribulation and the Antichrist   71

is on deception, presumably through false doctrine or philosophy. I think this adds weight to the idea that the man of lawlessness is someone who promotes a false doctrine or philosophy capable of performing counterfeit miracles. I spoke with a woman recently who was saved out of the New Age movement and she told me that she had seen some healing while she was in the movement. She is now involved in a full-time Christian healing ministry and said that what she saw previously is nothing compared to what she now witnesses through the power of the Holy Spirit. These verses in 2 Thessalonians place the emphasis on the man of lawlessness deceiving people rather than using physical persecution to achieve his goals. This is not a new tactic. Satan used this approach when he successfully seduced Adam and Eve to sin, and he tried the same tactic again when he tempted Jesus in the wilderness. He didn't use force on either of these occasions, but tried to deceive them by twisting what God had said.

- Matthew 24:24 may refer to the antichrist, as we have already noted. False Christs is another term for antichrists. Jesus tells us that they will "appear and perform great signs and miracles to deceive even the elect—if that were possible." These words of Jesus bear a striking similarity to Paul's description of the man of lawlessness whose coming "will be in accordance with the works of Satan displayed in all kinds of counterfeit miracles, signs and wonders." Again the emphasis is on deception rather that straight-out physical persecution.

- While I do not believe the Bible teaches that there will be a universal "great tribulation" immediately prior to Christ's return, and that it will be more intense than anything the church has ever experienced, we must not think that the church will live a peaceful existence. Jesus warned his disciples to expect persecution, and a study of church history reveals how accurate Jesus' predictions have been. We have already noted that in the 1990s around 300,000 people were martyred each year for being followers of Jesus. During the twentieth century, persecution has been intense in China, the USSR, Uganda, Islamic nations, and elsewhere. While those who live in Australia, the USA, and Western Europe have escaped intense physical persecution, there is no guarantee that this will continue; we have not been promised immunity from it. Persecution began back in the early chapters of the book of Acts and it will continue until Christ returns.

- Let me ask the question, Will we recognize the antichrist when he comes, assuming that he is a person who promotes a false doctrine and philosophy? Maybe and maybe not. It seems to me that there is sufficient evidence to say that he may be here already. Humanism, the New Age movement, the current promotion of atheism, and false doctrine that denies the basic message of salvation, are quite effective in achieving their goals. As I mentioned earlier, it is unlikely but possible that he has already been revealed and that Christ could return at any moment to destroy him.

- Finally, Jesus will destroy the antichrist when he returns. The mere presence of the glory of the risen Christ will be sufficient to "wipe him out" in an instant.

I lean towards the idea that the antichrist—the man of lawlessness—is someone who promotes a false doctrine or philosophy, and in that way tries to usurp the place of God. It is interesting to note that the only places in the Bible that refer to the antichrist by that name are the letters of John. Here the emphasis is clearly on false teaching and this gives weight to the idea that the antichrist is someone who promotes a false doctrine or philosophy, or that he is the philosophy itself. When we look at the church in Western Europe, for example, where the attack of the evil one has been more along the lines of humanistic philosophy and false liberal theology, and compare it with China, where Satan has used physical persecution to achieve his goals, one would have to conclude that deception in the West has been far more effective than physical persecution in China.

While I may not be certain as to who or what the antichrist is, I know that I am to live my life, either in peace or persecution, in a way that is prepared for the Lord to return. I need to be ready so that I will not be embarrassed when he comes. I have to live with eternal values in mind.

5

Our Resurrection Body

INTRODUCTION

THERE ARE CERTAIN THINGS we can't grasp with our finite minds about the resurrection body. For example:

- How can it be raised if it has been in the ground for over a thousand years and has totally decayed?
- How can it be capable of eating and drinking, as we will discuss shortly, but still be able to pass through solid objects such as doors and walls?
- How can it be immortal and not need food or drink to survive, even though it has the ability to eat and drink?

We don't know the answer to these questions for we are limited in our understanding of these areas. We do know that the resurrection body is a historical reality, for Jesus had one. We are not discussing something totally in the future, but something that over five hundred people have already seen; something that radically changed their lives: "that he was buried, that he was raised on the third day according to the Scriptures, and that he appeared to Peter, and then to the Twelve. After that, he appeared to more than five hundred of the brothers at the same time, most of whom are still living, though some have fallen asleep. Then he appeared to James, then to all the apostles, and last of all he appeared to me also, as to one abnormally born" (1 Cor 15:4–8). While we can't fully grasp how these things can happen, we know that the resurrection body is a certainty, for we have the proof in our Lord's resurrection body.

Let me say that just because we can't understand something, or because we haven't experienced something, doesn't mean that it doesn't exist. I like to tell people in Australia and Central Africa that I have walked across a lake which was over twenty meters deep for approximately a hundred meters with ordinary shoes and I didn't get wet. In other words, I have walked on water. Then I ask them if they believe me. They invariably say, "No!" But the truth is that I have, and it happened in Canada during the winter when it gets so cold that the lakes freeze over. I remember a Canadian missionary who served in Ethiopia, relating how he would tell the villagers that in his homeland it became so cold that the water in the lakes became so hard that you could walk on them, and that white flakes fell from the sky and covered the ground up to a meter or more. They didn't believe him and thought he was mad. Just because we have not seen something or can't imagine it, doesn't mean that it doesn't exist; it only shows that our experience and thinking is limited. The resurrection body is a historical reality.

WE RECEIVE OUR RESURRECTION BODY WHEN CHRIST RETURNS

Believers, those who have died, and those who are alive when Christ comes, will receive their resurrection bodies when he returns.

- 1 Thessalonians 4:14–17, "We believe that Jesus died and rose again and so we believe that God will bring with Jesus those who have fallen asleep in him. According to the Lord's own word, we tell you that we who are still alive, who are left till the coming of the Lord, will certainly not precede those who have fallen asleep. For the Lord himself will come down from heaven, with a loud command, with the voice of the archangel and with the trumpet call of God, and the dead in Christ will rise first. After that, we who are still alive and are left will be caught up together with them in the clouds to meet the Lord in the air. And so we will be with the Lord forever." We note here that the Lord will return to earth with the trumpet call of God and the dead in Christ will rise first.

- 1 Corinthians 15:51–53, "Listen, I tell you a mystery: We will not all sleep, but we will all be changed—in a flash, in the twinkling of an eye, at the last trumpet. For the trumpet will sound, the dead will be raised imperishable, and we will be changed. For the perishable must clothe itself with the imperishable, and the mortal with immortality." This also confirms that all believers, whether they have died or are still alive, will receive their resurrection bodies at the "trumpet call of God," that is, when Christ returns.

When we examine 1Thessalonians 4:14–17 we see a sequence of events. The souls/spirits of the believers who are presently in heaven with the Lord will come down with him. At this point in time, their physical bodies will be raised and transformed into an immortal, imperishable body so that the spirit/soul is reunited with the body, but now it is a renewed resurrection body. An instant after this, the believers who are still alive, will be caught up into the air and their bodies will be changed so that they also become imperishable. From this position "in the clouds," all believers will then return to the earth to reign with Christ during his millennium reign, and so they will be with the Lord forever.

OUR RESURRECTION BODY WILL BE LIKE CHRIST'S RESURRECTION BODY

There are a number of verses in Scripture that tell us that our resurrection body will be like Christ's glorious body. Consider the following:

- Philippians 3:20–21 "But our citizenship is in heaven. And we eagerly await a Savior from there, the Lord Jesus Christ, who, by the power that enables him to bring everything under his control, will transform our lowly bodies so that they will be like his glorious body."
- 1 Corinthians 15:49, "And just as we have borne the likeness of the earthly man, so shall we bear the likeness of the man from heaven."
- 1 John 3:2, "Dear friends, now we are children of God, and what we will be has not yet been made known. But we know that when he appears, we shall be like him, for we shall see him as he is."

CHRIST THE "FIRSTFRUITS" GUARANTEES OUR RESURRECTION BODY AND SHOWS US WHAT IT IS LIKE

Christ is sometimes referred to as the "firstfruits": "For as in Adam all die, so in Christ all will be made alive. But each in his own turn: Christ, the firstfruits; then, when he comes, those who belong to him" (1 Cor. 15:22–23). This is an agricultural term. In Leviticus 23:10 the Israelites were commanded to take the first sheaf of the harvest to the temple and offer it to God. I don't know if you have ever seen wheat being harvested, but it is an interesting experience. I lived for six years in the northwest wheat-belt of New South Wales, Australia. When it was time to harvest, the farmer would walk into his field and take a few heads of wheat. By looking at them, and by running certain tests, he could tell you how many tons he would harvest and what the quality would be like. If the "firstfruits," the first bunch of heads that are picked, are full and of premium quality, then he knows that the harvest will be good. Good "firstfruits" are a guarantee that there will be a good harvest. Paul uses this picture to teach that believers are the harvest, and we will have the same resurrection body as Christ, who is the "firstfruits."

Let me give you a modern illustration. Assume the company that makes BMWs publicly states that they will start production on a super car—but no date is given. The engine, which is powered by air, produces no pollution. There is no road noise or engine noise; it is totally quiet when travelling at 200kph. Furthermore, it has an autopilot override that anticipates potential problems, such as head-on collisions, and takes evasive action, thus eliminating the possibility of accidents. You may laugh and be skeptical, but if I took you to the factory and showed you the prototype in action—giving you the opportunity to drive it yourself—then you would believe that the company was telling the truth about this car.

Christ's resurrection body is the prototype. We can be certain that we will receive a similar body in the future. It is not a "pie in the sky" dream, but a reality based on the fact that hundreds of people have already seen it.

Flesh and Bone but Different

If we get an understanding of what Christ's resurrection body is like, then we gain a better insight into what our resurrection body will be like. The balance of this chapter will therefore look at Christ's resurrection body.

Luke 24:39 tells us that Jesus' resurrection body had "flesh and bone." He could be touched and held onto (Matt 28:9). Note also John 20:17.[1] While it had "flesh and bone" that could be touched, this "flesh

---

1. The KJV wrongly translates this as, "touch me not; for I am not yet ascended to my Father but go to my brethren," suggesting that his resurrection body was in an interim state and had to get a "protective coating" first. The NIV translates it correctly as "Do not hold on to me." The Greek construction is the negative *"ma"* plus the present imperative. This is a command to stop something already in progress. Jesus is telling

and bone" was different to what we have in our present natural body, for it seems to defy many of the present laws of physics. In John 20:19 and 26 Jesus suddenly appears in the room with the disciples even though the doors were locked. It is significant that John mentions twice that the "doors were locked," for I am sure that he wants us to know that the resurrection body is not subject to the same physical laws that govern our present, natural bodies. In a way we do not understand, Christ's body was able to pass through solid walls and ceilings.

I remember having a purely secular conversation with a work colleague about the ultimate form of travel. He suggested that it involved molecular reconstruction. If you wanted to go from point A to point B, the body would deconstruct itself, travel at the speed of light to point B, and then reconstruct itself immediately. We must be careful to note that the Bible doesn't say anything like this, nor does it tell us how Jesus could suddenly appear in the Upper Room when the doors were locked. However, I wouldn't be surprised if the resurrection body isn't capable of moving from point A to point B in a manner, and in a time frame, which defies our present understanding of the laws of physics. Concerning the characteristics of the resurrection body, Leon Morris writes, "It would seem that the risen Lord could conform to the limitations of this physical life or not as He chose, and this may indicate that when we rise we shall have a similar power."[2]

A Spiritual Body

First Corinthians 15:42–44 reads, "So will it be with the resurrection of the dead. The body that is sown is perishable, it is raised imperishable; it is sown in dishonor, it is raised in glory; it is sown in weakness, it is raised in power; it is sown a natural body, it is raised a spiritual body."

Paul tells us that our present body dies as a natural body, but our resurrection body is raised as a spiritual body. This doesn't mean that it is ghost-like, for we have seen that people were able to touch and hold onto Jesus' resurrection body, but it does tell us that it is different from our natural body and will be ideally suited to the spiritual world. Our present bodies are perishable but our resurrection body will be imperishable, that is, not capable of dying. Our existing bodies are sown in

---

Mary not to continue to cling onto him, for it will be many days before he ascends permanently to his father; rather, go and tell the disciples that he is alive.

2. Morris, "The Resurrection," 1089

dishonor and weakness, but our resurrection bodies will be raised in glory and power.

The Resurrection Body Can Eat and Drink but Doesn't Have to in Order to Stay Alive

The resurrection body is immortal and imperishable (1 Cor 15:50–54) and, therefore, cannot decay or die, even without food. However, while it doesn't need a regular intake of food and drink to stay alive, it is capable of eating and drinking: "He was not seen by all the people, but by witnesses whom God had already chosen—by us who ate and drank with him after he rose from the dead" (Acts 10:41). Refer also Luke 24:41–43 and Acts 1:4. These times of eating and drinking with Jesus in his resurrection body must have made a big impression on Peter for him to mention it in his sermon to Cornelius. I believe that when we have our resurrection bodies in the new heaven and new earth we will eat purely for the pleasure and enjoyment of it. I also believe, even though there isn't a Bible verse to confirm it, that the quality of this food will be beyond anything we have presently experienced.

It is interesting to note that Revelation 19:9 and Matthew 22:1–14; 25:1–13, use the imagery of a banquet to describe eternal life. I know that Revelation is written in an apocalyptic style and that the references in Matthew are parables, but I believe there is a reality behind these images. There is something about a good meal with friends that produces an extra dimension of fellowship and pleasure. I don't think it is unrelated that the Bible talks about eternal life in terms of a banquet and that the resurrection body is capable of eating food. Assuming that the marriage supper of the lamb is a time of eating and drinking, just imagine what a great time of celebration it is going to be.

Will We Look the Same in Our Resurrection Body?

In discussing the question, "What is the resurrection body like?" we need to ask, "Will we look the same in our resurrection body as we do in our present physical body? The Bible tells us that people didn't always recognize Jesus, suggesting that there was something different about his appearance.

- John 20:14. Mary Magdalene didn't initially realize that it was Jesus when he appeared to her at the tomb. Some have suggested that it was still dark and that is why she didn't recognize him, but there was sufficient light for her to think he was the gardener. Would a gardener have been there if it was still "pitch black"?

- John 21:1–14. The disciples didn't recognize the person on the beach with whom they were having the conversation until the miracle of the fish occurred. We could say that the light might have been dim and they were about ninety meters from land, and that is why they couldn't identify him from the boat. However, when they came ashore we read, "None of the disciples dared ask him, 'Who are you?' They knew it was the Lord." (Verse 12). This suggests that when they were face to face with Jesus there was something about his appearance that was different from how it had been in his pre-crucifixion state. Verse 14 is also fascinating, for it shows that the disciples were still puzzled about Jesus' physical looks even though they had seen him on two other occasions. "This was now the third time Jesus appeared to his disciples after he was raised from the dead."

- In Luke 24:13–16 the disciples on the Road to Emmaus didn't recognize him at first because they were kept from doing so. Later on (verse 31) they knew who Jesus was *"when their eyes were opened."* Does this mean the disciples needed special insight to identify Jesus because he looked slightly different? Like the previous story, was it something Jesus did or the way he did it that made them realize who he was? Was it the intimate way he addressed his father during grace, or did they see the scars on his hands when he broke the bread?

The evidence suggests that Jesus looked sufficiently different after the resurrection and the disciples didn't immediately recognize him.

If the resurrection body looks different to the "natural" body, and it appears that it does, how would it be different?

- Any birth deformities will be obliterated. These are the result of sin in the world; although they are not necessarily the result of the person's sin (John 9:1–3). Everything God created was good!

- The physical effect of sin on our bodies, which were caused by a sinful life, will be gone.

- The negative effects of aging on our bodies will disappear. We were not created to decay and die; this is also a result of sin in the world. This has prompted some people to say that our resurrection body will be that of a thirty-three year old, since that was the age of Jesus when he received his resurrection body. I don't find any direct support for this in the Scriptures, but I am confident that it will be a body of a person in his or her prime.

- It is probable that the effect of sin on the human race over the millenniums has so deformed the human body that it looks different from the body that Adam and Eve had when they were created.[3] In the early pages of the Bible we note that people lived considerably longer than they do now. Maybe the differences in appearance between the "natural" and "resurrection" bodies are due, in part, to the removal of the effects of that "gradual deforming process" of sin.

There will only be one person in the new heaven and new earth who has any scars on his body. They will be the nail-scarred hands and feet of our savior, plus his pierced side—a constant reminder of his overwhelming love for us.

More interesting questions are, "What will be the color of our skin? Will it bear any resemblance to what we have now?" The Bible doesn't tell us but these are interesting questions to ponder. I think that our resurrection body will have a skin color similar to what we have now. I have asked African pastors how they see their resurrection body and some of them envisage it as being a glowing white. I think many of them see themselves as being inferior and believe that they are under a curse of some kind. This is understable, for some white people, with their feelings of racial superiority, have made the Africans feel this way. I should also say that feelings of racial superiority are not limited to whites for black Africans from one tribe sometimes feel that they are superior to those from another. The whole concept of racial superiority is evidence of man's universal sinful nature. I know that God loves diversity, and I like to believe that when we get our resurrection bodies we will have different skin tones, but we will totally rejoice in the color

---

3. I am not talking about the impact of environment and culture, which results in an Italian looking different from a Scot or a Japanese person.

of our skin and marvel that, while we are all different, God has made us truly one.

I like this summary from Summers, "Apparently his body was so transformed and glorified that it had powers which transcended the ordinary operation of laws in the realm of the material and natural level of life. Once it had known the limitations of suffering and death. After the resurrection this was no longer true. Tangible—transcendent! In that seeming paradox the phenomenon must be left. As his precrucifixion body had been adapted to the needs of life in this world, so his resurrection body was adapted to the needs of the new plane of life. The reality of it is too sublime to be grasped by finite minds. There the writers of the New Testament left it; there must we leave it."[4] Hallelujah, our body will be like his glorious body!

---

4. Summers, *The Life Beyond*, 46

6

The Millennium

INTRODUCTION

THE DOCTRINE OF THE millennium, and the victorious reign of Christ, is primarily based on Revelation 20:1–6, and especially the latter part of verse 4, "They came to life and reigned with Christ a thousand years." Volumes have been written on these verses without any great consensus among Bible-believing scholars. This is one area of doctrine where we need to realize that we do not know it all and respect those who believe that the Bible is teaching something different than what we hold. There are four main views:

- postmillennialism
- dispensational premillennialism
- historic or classic premillennialism and
- amillennialism or realized millennialism

Postmillennialism teaches the following:

- This view sees the church as having such a profound influence on the world that evil is defeated and good reigns. It sees the church as completing the Great Commission so that the world is truly Christianized and, as a result of this, a period of peace and prosperity follows. Christ will be reigning spiritually through the church as it successfully completes the Great Commission and brings Christian values to every nation. This is the millennium.

- Near the end of the millennium, Christians will become lax and Satan will reassert himself and try to get people to follow him.

- At this point Christ will return and usher in the eternal state.
- "Post" means "after," and so "postmillennialism" means that Christ will return after the millennial reign of peace and prosperity that is brought on by the complete spread of the gospel.

Dispensational premillennialism advocates the following:
- This view sees the second coming as two events separated by a period of time, usually seven years, although some say it will be three and a half years. The first phase is a secret rapture where the believers are taken to heaven to be with Christ and to enjoy the "marriage supper of the lamb."
- While the believers are in heaven, the earth will go through the great tribulation when God will pour out his wrath on the world. This view is also known as "Pretribulationism" because the church will be removed from the earth before (pre) the "great tribulation." The antichrist will appear during this time.
- Christ will then return to the earth with his saints and they will receive their resurrection bodies and reign with him on earth. This is the millennium.
- Satan will be bound and thrown into the abyss at the beginning of the millennium but released for a little while at the end of it. Satan will then be totally defeated and the millennial reign of Christ will end, the final judgment will take place, and the final state will be introduced.

Historic premillennialism, which is different from dispensational premillennialism, maintains that:
- The second coming of Christ is a single event rather than two separated by seven years.
- The saints receive their resurrection bodies when Christ returns, and they reign with him on this earth. This is the millennium.
- Satan will be bound and thrown into the abyss at the beginning of the millennium but released for a little while at the end of it. Satan will then be totally defeated and the millennial reign of Christ will end, the final judgment will take place, and the final state will be introduced.

Amillennialism or realized millennialism, can be summarized as follows:

- Christ is reigning on earth now because the kingdom of God is a present reality, and we are not to look forward to a literal, bodily reign of Christ on earth after his return, hence the prefix "A," meaning "none." I prefer the term "realized millennialism" over "amillennialism" because the latter suggests that these people do not believe in the millennium. They do, but they place it between the resurrection of Christ and his second coming. They argue that the thrones are in heaven (Rev 1:4; 3:21; 4:1ff), and therefore this is a spiritual reign rather than an earthly physical reign. It is a reign that is currently taking place in the heavenlies.

- The second coming of Christ immediately ushers in the eternal state, that is, the final judgment, hell, and the new heaven and new earth.

- They believe that the binding of Satan, as mentioned in Revelation 20:2, was accomplished by Christ through his life and death (Matt 12:25–29; Col 2:15). Satan, because he is bound, cannot stop the church from growing and achieving what God has planned for her. This is in stark contrast to the Old Testament where he was easily able to stop any advances to the kingdom of God. For example, in Nineveh the people repented at the preaching of Jonah but history shows that the "faith" soon disappeared.

- The first resurrection is understood in a couple of ways. It could refer to the new birth when we cross from death to life, and, as a result of this, believers reign with Christ in the heavenly realms (John 5:25; Eph 2:5–6). The more common interpretation is that it refers to the believers who have been martyred; they may have been physically killed, but their souls have risen to God and are now reigning with Christ in heaven.

- Amillenialists would argue that outside of this difficult passage, the New Testament never speaks of an earthly messianic reign; therefore the obscure passages, such as Revelation 20:1–4, should be interpreted by the clearer passages; that is, they should be interpreted in harmony with the teachings of the entire Bible.[1]

Each view has had a period of history when it has been more popular than others, and this often has to do with the state of the world at that time. Interestingly, a belief in an earthly, physical reign of Christ, that is, the premillennial view, was condemned as "superstitious" by the Council of Ephesus in AD 431.[2]

WHICH IS MORE BIBLICALLY CORRECT?

As I mentioned earlier, Bible-believing scholars genuinely hold to different views on the topic while some godly church leaders can't come down definitively on one side. I remember listening to a great man of God, who had pastored a number of large influential churches in the USA and UK, and who was the author of many books, trying to answer the question as to what view he held. He admitted that he couldn't decide, for when he listened to a particular person advocating one view he thought that he or she was right, but when he listened to another person explaining another view, he thought that person was correct.

I was raised on the dispensational premillennial view and didn't know that Bible-believing Christians could hold to anything else and still believe in the authority of the Bible. It came as quite a shock to me when I met a very godly Bible-believing pastor who was a strong advocate for the inerrancy of the Bible, but who also held to the amillennial view. I have now rejected the dispensational view for a number of reasons, but primarily they are:

- I disagree with the whole concept of dispensations, and especially that it is only this present church-age that is the "age of grace." The book of Romans teaches that man has always been made right

---

1. Hendriksen, *More than Conquerors*, 49. He writes, "In emphasizing this basis of the Apocalyptic visions in the subsoil of the sacred Scriptures we must always bear in mind that it is wise to proceed from the clearer to the more obscure and never *vice versa*. This has often been forgotten. A passage which by itself is rather obscure is seized on; for example, Revelation 20:2. It is given a most literal interpretation. Then—to cap the climax—all the clear passages in the more didactic portions of Scripture are distorted in such a fashion that they will agree with the meaning which the 'interpreter' has poured into the obscure passage ... The *Apocalypse is rooted in the sacred Scriptures. It should be interpreted in harmony with the teachings of the entire Bible.* (Emphasis in original.)

2. Clouse, *The Meaning of the Millennium*, 9.

with God by faith in him. Regardless of whether we are speaking about Abraham, David, or us, we are only ever saved by grace through faith; there is no other way and there has never been any other way and there never will be any other way. If there could be any other way for man to be right with God, then Christ didn't have to die.

- I disagree that the church is a parenthesis in God's plan that only came into existence because the Jews rejected Jesus. The church is the goal of God's strategy in the world; it is the body of Christ and it comprises both Jews and Gentiles. Those who repent and put their faith in Christ will spend eternity with him in the new heaven and new earth, but those who reject him, be they Jew or Gentile, will be sent to hell.

- I cannot see that the second coming of Christ is in two stages separated by a number of years.

I also reject the postmillennial view because I don't think it makes the best sense of Scripture, and it probably came into prominence in the eighteenth century because it agreed with the prevailing thought of the Enlightenment. I have to admit that I like the optimism of this view, for it takes the power of God to transform people and society seriously. It is a welcome relief from the dispensational view, which is particularly pessimistic about God's power in this regard.

This leaves us with either the amillennial position or the historic premillennial view. For many years I was unable to decide and would sometimes swing from favoring one to slightly favoring the other. However, I have now come down on the side of the historic premillennial view, mainly because of what we learn from church history. Let me elaborate my thinking in this regard.

- The New Testament is the final, complete revelation from God. We must start any doctrinal study by asking, what did Jesus and the apostles teach? Hebrews tells us that the "reality" is in the New Covenant while the Old Covenant is only the "shadows." If we start with the Old Testament, we begin by looking at the shadows and are likely to get it wrong; we must start with the New Testament and then look into the Old Testament for further insight. If we only had the New Testament, I would probably favor the amillennial view slightly, for I think this makes the most sense of the New Testament. It is simple and straightforward and lacks the problems associated with the premillennial view. We need to note that there is no clear reference in the New Testament to an earthly reign of Christ outside of Revelation 20 and these verses are in a book that is written in a style that we are not accustomed to. The amillennial understanding of Revelation as "progressive parallelism"[3] is acceptable.

- The Old Testament, on the surface, favors the premillennial view because there are verses which look forward to a golden age when the messiah will reign, resulting in peace and prosperity for all, but that falls short of the eternal state. Zechariah 14:5–19 is a good example of this. This passage in Zechariah can't refer to the present time for verse 9 tells us that, "The LORD will be king over the whole earth. On that day there will be one LORD and his name the only name," but it doesn't refer to the eternal state in the new heaven and new earth either, for some of the inhabitants rebel against the Lord and they are punished with plagues and lack of rain. It best fits the earthly millennial reign of Christ.

Ladd also sees support for the premillennial view in Ezekiel's prophecy in chapters 36–37. He writes,

> While the New Testament has little to say about a temporal messianic kingdom, Ezekiel's prophecy has the same basic structure as Rev 20. Chapters 36–37 picture the salvation of Israel, restored to their land and blessed with the messianic salvation (see 36:24–29). The goal of prophetic expectation, "you shall be my people, and I will be your God" (Ezek 36:28) is now realized. David, God's servant, will rule over his people, and God

---

3. Progressive Parallelism claims that the book of Revelation has seven distinct sections and each begins with the first coming of Christ and goes to the end. The seven sections therefore run parallel to each other and progressively give us more detail on a given matter. For example, the final judgment is first "announced" in the early chapters, but as the book unfolds it is then "introduced" and finally "described" in more detail. Similarly, the new heaven and earth is described more fully in the final section than in those which precede it. On this basis, Revelation 20:1 is seen as the start of a new section which takes us back to the physical life of Christ. The binding of Satan (Rev 20:2) occurred during the life of Jesus, commencing with his victory in the wilderness temptations (Matt 4:1–11) and culminating with his victory on the cross (Col 2:15). Because of this binding, Satan can no longer deceive the nations as he had done in the Old Testament time. He is now powerless to stop the spread of the gospel. Refer to William Hendriksen, *More than Conquerors: An Interpretation of the Book of Revelation*.

will dwell in their midst (37:25,28). However, the blessing of the messianic kingdom is not the end. The kingdom is disturbed by an eschatological war led by Gog from Magog (chapters 38–39); and only after divine victory do we have a picture of the eternal new order, which in Ezekiel is described in terms of a rebuilt temple in the new Jerusalem (chapters 40–48). This structure of a temporal kingdom, followed by the eternal kingdom in the new age, is the same as that in Revelation.[4]

However, we must note that the apostles, and presumably Jesus, often interpreted the Old Testament spiritually rather than literally, and saw the promises that related to physical Israel as being fulfilled in the church.[5] The Old Testament doesn't rule out the amillennial position, but it does seem to favor the premillennial view.

- While the Bible is our supreme source of authority in all matters of faith and doctrine, a study of church history helps us to understand more fully the teaching of the Bible. It seems that the premillennial view was the dominant view of the church fathers, who immediately followed the apostles. People such as Papias, Irenaeus, Justin Martyr, and Tertullian taught a premillennial position,[6] although they say nothing about a secret rapture with a seven-year interval between it and the return of Christ. The amillennial view doesn't appear to have been accepted until the fifth century, when it was popularized by Augustine (AD 354–430).[7] It seems to me that the greater the time between the writing of the New Testament and the introduction of a certain teaching, the less likely it is that this view is what the apostles taught. The fact that the early fathers immediately following the apostles taught a premillennial view is an overwhelming argument, and is the reason why I hold to the historic premillennial view, although I must say "with reservations" because it is not without its problems.

---

4. Ladd, *Revelation of John*, 269–70.

5. In Acts 15:12–18 James says that the church, both Jew and Gentile, is the fulfillment of Amos 9:11–12, but these verses in Amos talk about the restoration of the nation of Israel. In Romans 9:24–26, Paul sees the church as the fulfillment of Hosea 1:10–11; 2:23, but in their original context they refer to physical Israel.

6. Clouse, *The Meaning of the Millennium*, 9.

7. Mounce, writes, "It was Augustine, however, who about the beginning of the fifth century made the first serious effort to interpret Revelation 20 in a non-millenarian fashion" (*The Book of Revelation*, 358).

THE HISTORIC PREMILLENNIAL VIEW

The balance of this chapter will advocate a historic premillennial position, based on the assumption from church history that the apostles taught a "premillennial view."

Revelation 20:1–6

> And I saw an angel coming down out of heaven, having the key to the Abyss and holding in his hand a great chain. He seized the dragon, that ancient serpent, who is the devil, or Satan, and bound him for a thousand years. He threw him into the Abyss, and locked and sealed it over him, to keep him from deceiving the nations anymore until the thousand years were ended. After that, he must be set free for a short time. (Rev 20:1–3)
>
> I saw thrones on which were seated those who had been given authority to judge. And I saw the souls of those who had been beheaded because of their testimony for Jesus and because of the word of God. They had not worshiped the beast or his image and had not received his mark on their foreheads or their hands. They came to life and reigned with Christ a thousand years. (The rest of the dead did not come to life until the thousand years were ended.) This is the first resurrection. Blessed and holy are those who have part in the first resurrection. The second death has no power over them, but they will be priests of God and of Christ and will reign with him for a thousand years (Rev 20:4–6)

These verses are the only definite reference to the millennium in the New Testament, and so it is crucial that we examine them in some detail. The first thing we need to note is their immediate context.

- Revelation 19:6–10 announces the marriage supper of the lamb, where the bride will be united with Christ, the bridegroom.
- Revelation 19:11–21 describes the second coming of Christ. He comes as the victorious conqueror who is "King of kings and Lord of lords." These verses describe how Christ defeats the beast and the false prophet. (This is the battle of Armageddon that was announced back in Rev 16:12–16.) However, while the forces of evil gather to make war against Christ, none are described. Instead we read that the beast and false prophet were captured and thrown into the fiery lake of burning sulfur, and that the rest were killed

by the sword in Christ's mouth. This passage doesn't describe a battle that wages back and forth, but a victory that is gained in an instant. It is the splendor of Christ's presence that destroys his enemies.

The argument for the premillennial position is that Revelation 20:1–10 naturally follows from chapter 19 and describes the total defeat of Satan, who is the power behind the beast and the false prophet. This victory occurs in two stages. First, Satan is bound when Christ returns, and Satan is thrown into the abyss for a thousand years to stop him from deceiving the nations, as he had done through the beast (Rev 20:3). At the end of this period, he is released for a short time (verse 3) before he is finally defeated by Christ and thrown into the lake of burning sulfur (Rev 20:10).

Revelation 19:11—20:15 give us a sequential series of events:

- The first is the return of Christ, which results in the beast and the false prophet being thrown into the lake of fire.
- Satan is then bound for a thousand years while Christ begins his millennial reign on earth.
- At the end of the thousand years, Satan is released for a little while and gathers the nations to make war against God.
- Satan is captured and thrown into the lake of fire.
- The final judgment begins.

Vital to our understanding of Revelation 20:1-6 is the meaning of the Greek verb, *ezesan*, which is used twice in verses 4 and 5 and translated "came to life" and "do not come to life." What does it refer to? Revelation 20:4-5 tells us that there are two resurrections: one which takes place at the beginning of the millennium, and the other which occurs at the end of it. Before proceeding I need to note that most Bible-believing scholars maintain that unbelievers will be raised from the dead in their old sinful bodies at the final judgment.[8] This will happen at the end of the millennium and immediately prior to the final judgment. People who hold to the amillennial view or to the premillennial view usually agree on this. The point of difference relates to the "first resurrection" which occurs at the beginning of the millennium; is this a bodily

---

8. In Matthew 10:28 Jesus tells us that both soul and body will be destroyed in hell. This implies that the unbeliever is raised in his old body to face the final judgment.

resurrection as the premillennialist maintains, or a spiritual resurrection as the amillennialist teaches? The answer to this question has a major bearing on what view we hold to.

There is no doubt that Scripture talks about a spiritual resurrection (Eph 2:1-6) while some passages, such as John 5:25-29, mention both a spiritual and a bodily resurrection, but the context of these passages show how they should be interpreted. However, the context of Revelation 20:1-6 does not give us any indication that *ezesan* (came to life) in Revelation 20:4 should be translated differently from that in verse 5. Since verse 5 refers to a physical resurrection, we must understand verse 4 as also referring to a physical resurrection. This is the premillennial view. It seems to be a distortion of language to get one verb to refer to a spiritual resurrection and the other to a physical resurrection, which is the amillennial understanding, when there is no indication that one is supposed to be translated differently from the other.

In summary, we can say that Revelation 20:1-6 continues on from Revelation 19 and shows the sequence of events that occur when Christ returns to earth. Revelation 20:1-6 tells us that Satan will be bound and thrown into the abyss—this is different from hell—for the period of the millennium. The dead believers will be physically raised with their resurrection bodies, and they, along with the transformed believers who were alive at the time of Christ's return, will reign with Christ on earth during the millennium. At the end of this period Satan will be let loose and will gather the nations to war against God, but they will be destroyed, and Satan himself will be thrown into the lake of burning sulfur.

Other Verses in New Testament Relating to the Millennium

Refer to 1 Corinthians 15:23-25, "But each in his own turn: Christ, the firstfruits; then, when he comes, those who belong to him. Then the end will come, when he hands over the kingdom to God the Father after he has destroyed all dominion, authority and power. For he must reign until he has put all his enemies under his feet." The two Greek adverbs translated "then" denote a sequence of three stages. The first is the resurrection of Christ—he is the "firstfruits"—then, after a period of time, the saints will be resurrected at the return of Christ, then, after another period of time, the end, that is, the final eternal state. Paul talks about a period of time between the second coming of Christ and the final state, and this is exactly when the millennium fits.

I infer a reference to the premillennial view in 2 Thessalonians 2:1–2. The Thessalonian believers, who were well-taught on matters pertaining to the second coming, thought that it was possible for them to be left behind on the present earth after Christ had returned, hence their concern. The only view that allows for this possibility is the premillennial one. Paul's reply is also interesting because he seems to suggest that this is how it will be, and hence he talks about the man of lawlessness. If he held to an amillennial view, then surely he would have told the Thessalonians that it was impossible for them to still be on the earth after Christ's return, since the parousia would introduce the final judgment and the eternal state. The premillennial view is the only one that seems to do justice to Paul's teaching in 2 Thessalonians 2.

John 5:24–29 may also support the premillennial position. Verses 24–25 refer to a present resurrection: "I tell you the truth, whoever hears my word and believes him who sent me has eternal life and will not be condemned; he has crossed over from death to life. I tell you the truth, a time is coming and has now come when the dead will hear the voice of the Son of God and those who hear will live." This resurrection is a spiritual resurrection and refers to the new birth that the believer receives when he passes from spiritual death to spiritual life. This resurrection is available now for "the hour is coming and now is" and it has been available for almost two thousand years since Jesus uttered these words. Verses 28–29 refer to a future resurrection, "Do not marvel at this; for an hour is coming, in which all who are in the tombs shall hear His voice, and shall come forth; those who did the good deeds to a resurrection of life, those who committed the evil deeds to a resurrection of judgment." (NASB) This refers to the physical resurrection of the body.

While Jesus refers to two physical resurrections in John 5:29—people who did good deeds being raised to a resurrection of life and people who committed evil deeds to a resurrection of judgment—the question needs to be asked if they occur simultaneously or if there is a substantial period of time between them. If it is the former then it supports the amillennial teaching, but if it is the latter then it confirms the premillennial position. The context gives us a clue. The hour in John 5:24–25 is not a point in time, but an extended period of time, and, as we have noted, has lasted almost two thousand years and still going. Since "the hour" in verse 25 covers an extended period of time rather than a point in time, it is not unreasonable to say that "the hour" in verse 28, when the dead "shall hear His voice," also covers an extended period. That is, there is a long period of time between the resurrection of the dead believers to life and the resurrection of the wicked dead to judgment. This is the same sequence of events that we note in Revelation 20:1–4. The believers are raised in their resurrection bodies at the beginning of the millennium while the unbelievers are not resurrected until the end of the millennium.

SATAN IS BOUND DURING THE MILLENNIUM

Revelation 20:3 tells us that Satan is bound and thrown into the abyss which is locked and sealed, so that he can not deceive the nations. The language of this verse suggests that Satan and his demons will be rendered completely inoperative. It is not a curbing of his activities but a complete stop to them. I believe this means that people will not be tempted to sin, which is one reason why Christ's reign on earth will bring peace and prosperity. However, Satan will be released at the end of the millennium, and he will again become active and be successful in deceiving people so that they follow him and rebel against God.

FULFILLMENT OF ROMANS 11:25–26

> I do not want you to be ignorant of this mystery, brothers, so that you may not be conceited: Israel has experienced a hardening in part until the full number of the Gentiles has come in. And so all Israel will be saved, as it is written:
> "The deliverer will come from Zion;
> he will turn godlessness away from Jacob." (Rom 11:25–26)

These verses show that there will be a time when all of the Jews who are alive on the earth (or at least the vast majority), will turn to Christ and be saved.[9] In the earlier verses Paul has used the figure of the olive tree to represent the people of God; the Jews are the natural branches and the Gentiles are the wild branches. The Gentiles have been grafted into the olive tree (the people of God), while the natural branches (the Jews) have

---

9. Bruce, writes, "'All Israel' is a recurring expression in Jewish literature, where it need not mean 'every Jew without a single exception', but 'Israel as a whole'. Thus 'all Israel has a portion in the age to come', says the Mishnah tractate *Sanhedrin* (10.1), and proceeds immediately to name certain Israelites who have no portion therein" (*The Letter of Paul to the Romans*, 209).

been cut off through unbelief. However, Paul tells us that God will graft the Jews back into his family if they turn to Christ in faith—if they do not continue in their unbelief: "And if they do not persist in unbelief, they will be grafted in, for God is able to graft them in again" (verse 23). The above tells us that a hardening has come upon a large part of Israel, for only a minority have acknowledged Jesus as the promised messiah, but when the full number of the Gentiles has come in, all Israel will be saved.

The context demands that we understand Israel as being the physical nation of Israel rather than spiritualizing it to represent the church. Israel in verse 25 is the nation of Israel, and there seems no valid reason from this passage to see Israel in verse 26 as referring to anything other than the nation of Israel.

While the New Testament doesn't give us any detail about when "all Israel will be saved," it would fit nicely into the millennial period. According to Romans 11:25–26, it will happen when "the full number of the Gentiles [have] come in," and this seems to be an apt description of the second coming of Christ. In Romans 11:26 Paul quotes from Isaiah 59:20, "The deliverer will come from Zion; he will turn godlessness away from Jacob," again suggesting that this conversion of Israel is associated with the coming of Christ. It suggests that the return of Jesus will make Israel, as a whole, acknowledge him as their messiah, and put their faith in him. If this is so, then Israel during the millennial reign of Christ, will become the world's first truly Christian nation.

When Scripture says, "and so all Israel will be saved," it doesn't refer to every Jew who has ever lived, but only to those who are alive at that point in history and who repent of their sin and put their faith in Jesus. We noted above in Romans 11:23 that the natural olive branches (the Jewish people) will be grafted back into the olive tree (the people of God) if they "do not persist in unbelief"; that is, they will become part of God's family, the "True Israel," when they repent and put their faith in Christ. Paul makes it very clear that Jews, like Gentiles, are only saved if they turn to God in repentance and trust Jesus for salvation. Acts 20:21 summarizes Paul's message well, "I have declared to both Jews and Greeks that they must turn to God in repentance and have faith in our Lord Jesus." There is not one message for Gentiles and a different one for Jews.

I was taught as a youth that all Jews, regardless of what era they have lived in, will be saved because they are God's chosen people.[10] This

---

10. This was not an uncommon belief among the Jews in the first century. Leon

is not what Paul is teaching in Romans 11:11–24, and it is certainly not what he is advocating throughout the book of Romans. The Jews are not right with God simply because they have Abraham as their father; they need to have the faith of Abraham. Yes, there are advantages in being a Jew, just as there are advantages in being raised in a Christian home, but ultimately a person will only escape hell if they have repented and put their faith in Christ. A person's ancestry doesn't make them right with God. "All Israel will be saved," means that a time is coming in history when all the Jews who are alive at that time, or at least the vast majority of them, will repent of their sin and believe in the Lord Jesus Christ.

Some see the conversion of the Jews as occurring in this age rather than in the millennium. They see it as a sign pointing to the nearness of Christ's return. I can't agree with this, for we could easily look at Israel to see how close the Lord's return is by examining how many Jews have been saved. This seems to be contrary to Jesus' teaching that his coming will be like a "thief in the night"; one doesn't know when the thief is going to come.

THE PURPOSE OF THE MILLENNIUM

Scripture doesn't tell us what the purpose of the millennium is, but scholars have made a number of suggestions.

- It is necessary so that Christ can put all his enemies under his feet (1 Cor 15:25).

- Christ's present reign is invisible and unrecognized by the world as a whole. The millennium will reveal to the world the glory and power of Christ's reign.

- Another reason is to highlight the justice of God at the final judgment. After the millennium, Satan will be released for a short time, and men and women will follow him, even though they have experienced the blessings of peace and prosperity under the reign

---

Morris writes, "The Jew seems to have combined two attitudes, one which stressed the community and the other the individual. He thought of his nation as the community of the saved. When he stood before God it was not simply as an individual, to be dealt with on the grounds of his personal record in keeping or not keeping the law. He belonged to God's own people and would be saved along with the rest of that people. His circumcision placed him firmly within the saved community. He might be punished for his sins, but he would not be eternally lost, for 'All Israelites have a share in the world to come' (Sanh. 10:1)." (*The Epistle to the Romans,* 108). This is one of the views that Paul argues against in Romans.

of Christ. Humankind at the final judgment will therefore have no excuse for their sinfulness. They will not be able to blame their rebellion against God on an evil society or a bad environment, but will see that it was their own choice and that they deserve the consequences of their actions.

HOW LONG IS THE MILLENNIUM?

This may initially seem like a stupid question, for the millennium means "a thousand," and Revelation 20:4 tells us that the believer reigns with Christ for a thousand years. However, Revelation is written in the style of Jewish apocalyptic literature with its vivid symbols, a fact that we acknowledge throughout the book. For example, in Revelation 17:9 we read, "This calls for a mind with wisdom. The seven heads are seven hills on which the woman sits." Here we are told that "heads" represents "hills" and that a woman sits on them. If we insist on taking everything literally then it would be a very big woman if she could sit on seven hills, but, of course, that is not how one is meant to understand apocalyptic literature. The woman who sits on the seven hills is Rome, both first-century Rome and any city that sets itself up against God. It is a vivid symbol.

Likewise, the 144,000 in Revelation 7:1–8 refers, not to literal Israel, for this list doesn't match any list of Israelite tribes in the Old Testament.[11] It is a symbolic number that refers to the true people of God, those who have the faith of Abraham: the church. Here 144,000 is not to be understood as literally 12,000 people from twelve tribes, but as the church—a great multitude that no one can count. The number is a symbol. Twelve (Old Testament saints) times twelve (New Testament saints) equals 144. Multiply this by one thousand, the symbol of completeness, and you have 144,000—the church, the true Israel, the people of God.

Now back to the question, "How long is the millennium?" As I have just mentioned, one thousand is ten times ten times ten, a symbol of

---

11. Ladd, *The Revelation of John*, 114–15. "As a matter of fact, John's list agrees with no known list of the enumeration of the twelve tribes of Israel." Ladd then compares Revelation 7 with Genesis 49 and Ezekiel 48 and concludes, "No satisfactory explanation of this irregular list of names has been offered, unless it be this: John intends to say that the twelve tribes of Israel are not really literal Israel, but the true, spiritual Israel—the church."

completeness.[12] A thousand, in the context of Revelation's apocalyptic literature, is a symbol of completeness rather than a literal thousand years.[13] When the time is complete, not before and not after, for God is in total control, he will let Satan loose and then bring about his final and complete destruction in the lake of fire. How long does God need to achieve what he wants to achieve in the reign of Christ on earth? I don't know and Scripture doesn't tell us, but does it have to be any more than, say, thirty to forty years? I know that this presents a problem if we are to take Isaiah 65:20 literally as referring to the millennium—"Never again will there be in it an infant who lives but a few days, or an old man who does not live out his years; he who dies at a hundred will be thought a mere youth; he who fails to reach a hundred will be considered accursed"—but a shorter period of thirty to forty years would allow the principles of this passage to be proven. I mean by this that Christ could show that infant mortality was the result of greed, indifference, and lack of knowledge, so that when these issues are addressed in a righteousness manner, premature infant death could be overcome. This would show that people no longer have to die in infancy or die prematurely when sin is removed from the equation.

One of the problems that I have with premillennialism concerns people coming to faith in Christ. The first question one has to ask is, "Can people, who were alive when Christ returned, be saved during the millennium, especially if they had heard the gospel previously and rejected it?" Scripture doesn't tell us, but if people are to be made right with God, the clear teaching of Romans and other books in the New Testament, is that they can only come into this relationship by faith. This applies to the Old Testament saints like Abraham and David who lived before the death of Christ (refer to Romans 4), and it applies to Gentiles and Jews alike who live after the death of Christ; there is no other way. We cannot work for salvation by showing good deeds to people, be they Jews or Gentiles; it is by faith in God and faith alone. Faith requires a degree of trust, and it is difficult to see how faith is required in the millennium if people see the risen Christ and the saints in their resurrection bodies.

12. Morris, *The Book of Revelation*, 229.
13. Ladd, *Revelation*, 262, writes, "It is difficult to understand the **thousand years** for which he was bound with strict literalness in view of the obvious symbolic use of numbers in the Revelation." (*Revelation*, 262) (Emphasis in original).

Maybe one of the reasons behind the release of Satan is to test the allegiance of those who have turned to Christ during this stage. A short period of time, say thirty to forty years, would minimize my problem for people who were saved after the return of Christ, if that is how God has planned it. They would still be alive when Satan was released—I am assuming that people live longer in the millennium (Isa. 65:20)—and this would give them an opportunity to prove the genuineness of their commitment to Jesus.

7

Judgment

THE CERTAINTY OF JUDGMENT

I REMEMBER WATCHING A news report on TV that showed a man, who had been charged with a particularly heinous crime, being driven away from the court under police protection. As the TV camera scanned the large crowd that had gathered, my attention was drawn to a woman who was holding a sign that read, "Burn in Hell." There is something within the human spirit that demands justice. We find it wrong that people can deliberately commit a crime and never have to face judgment with the appropriate punishment, especially if they use their wealth or influence to avoid it.

The Bible mentions judgment many times. God's justice demands that people can't deliberately rebel against him without having to give an account for their sin. Consider the following.

- Matthew 12:36, "But I tell you that men will have to give account on the day of judgment for every careless word they have spoken."
- Romans 14:10b, 12, "For we will all stand before God's judgment seat . . . So then, each of us will give an account of himself to God."
- Acts 17:31, "For he has set a day when he will judge the world with justice by the man he has appointed. He has given proof of this to all men by raising him from the dead."

JUDGMENT OF UNBELIEVERS

Judgment has two main purposes for the unbeliever.

- First, it will show that they have sinned and come short of God's standard, and hence deserve death.
- It also determines the degree of "torment" that one deserves in hell. We will discuss this in the following chapter.

We need to understand that judgment is always based on what we have done. It is based on our works, as the following shows.

- Revelation 20:12, "And I saw the dead, great and small, standing before the throne, and books were opened. Another book was opened, which is the book of life. The dead were judged according to what they had done as recorded in the books."
- Matthew 16:27, "For the Son of Man is going to come in his Father's glory with his angels, and then he will reward each person according to what he has done."
- 2 Corinthians 5:10, "For we must all appear before the judgment seat of Christ, that each one may receive what is due him for the things done while in the body, whether good or bad."

The fact that judgment is based on our deeds was a problem for me in my early years, for I could not reconcile it with the fact that eternal life is something we receive by faith. My problem centered on the fact that I erroneously thought that the purpose of judgment was to see if a person was "good enough" before God. I thought that people were judged to see if their good deeds outweighed their bad or something like that. I saw it like a school exam, where you had to do enough good to earn a passing mark. This is not the purpose of judgment for the unbeliever.

Judgment is to see if the individual has sinned and come short of the glory or standard of God. James tells us that one sin is sufficient to make us a sinner, and he uses the sin of showing favoritism to the rich over the poor to prove his point: "But if you show favoritism, you sin and are convicted by the law as lawbreakers. For whoever keeps the whole law and yet stumbles at just one point is guilty of breaking all of it" (James 2:9–10). This is difficult for religious people to grasp, for such people usually want to see themselves as being acceptable to God because of their good deeds. There is no such thing as being, say, 60 percent "not guilty" and only 40 percent "guilty"; we are all 100 percent guilty because we have all sinned at some stage in our life. Revelation 20:12–15 confirms this teaching of James. It shows that no one escapes being thrown into the lake of fire as a result of being judged. No one's works are good enough to save him or her; all are shown to be guilty. It is only those whose names are in the book of life who escape. It is only those who have repented of their sin, put their faith in Christ, and have received eternal life, who will be saved from God's wrath: "Whoever believes in the Son has eternal life, but whoever rejects the Son will not see life, for God's wrath remains on him" (John 3:36).

Paul tells us that when the unbeliever stands before the great white throne and is judged according to what is what he has done "as recorded in the books," he will realize that God is just in his judgment and that there is nothing the unbeliever can say in his defense: "Now we know that whatever the law says, it says to those who are under the law, so that every mouth may be silenced and the whole world held accountable to God" (Rom 3:19).

While every unbeliever will be found guilty and thrown into the lake of fire, there will be varying degrees of "torment"—for want of a better word—as a result of the judgment process: "But I tell you that it will be more bearable for Sodom on the day of judgment than for you" (Matt 11:24). I don't know exactly how God will vary the "torment," but I will discuss this matter further in the chapter on hell.

I find a parallel in our human courts of law. The prisoner is brought before the judge to ascertain if he is guilty of the crime as charged. It is not to see if his good deeds outweighed his bad, but to ascertain if the particular charge is valid. The judge, when considering his sentence, may vary the punishment depending on other circumstances, but a person who deliberately committed murder is a murderer, regardless of how many acts of kindness he may have done towards others.

BELIEVERS WILL BE JUDGED

Believers will also be judged according to their works, and this will occur at the final judgment as shown in Revelation 20:11–15. However, the believer can have the assurance that he will spend eternity with God in the new heaven and new earth rather than being thrown into the lake of fire. This is not because his works show that he is "good enough," but because his name is written in the book of life.

Paul also talks about the believer being judged:

- Romans 14:10,12, "You, then, why do you judge your brother? Or why do you look down on your brother? For we will all stand before God's judgment seat . . . So then, each of us will give an account of himself to God."
- 2 Corinthians 5:10, "For we must all appear before the judgment seat of Christ, that each one may receive what is due him for the things done while in the body, whether good or bad."

Some people want to make a distinction between "God's judgment seat" and the "judgment seat of Christ" and see them as two separate judgments, but there is little evidence to support this. Since Jesus is the one who is going to judge, and since Jesus is also fully God, it seems to me that both passages refer to the one final judgment. I do not find multiple judgments in the New Testament.

While the final judgment will be a fearful thing for unbelievers, believers do not have to dread it, but can look forward to it with confidence because their names are in the book of life. John tells us that we can have confidence on the day of judgment (1 John 4:17). One of the reasons for this is that, "there is now no condemnation for those who are in Christ Jesus, because through Christ Jesus the law of the Spirit of life set me free from the law of sin and death" (Rom 8:1–2).

JUDGMENT WILL DETERMINE OUR REWARDS

The primary reason for the judgment of believers is to reward them for their Christian service: "The time has come for judging the dead, and for rewarding your servants the prophets and your saints and those who reverence your name, both small and great—and for destroying those who destroy the earth" (Rev 11:18). We see this concept of rewards in other passages of Scripture as well.

- 1 Corinthians 3:8, "The man who plants and the man who waters have one purpose, and each will be rewarded according to his own labor."
- Ephesians 6:7–8, "Serve wholeheartedly, as if you were serving the Lord, not men, because you know that the Lord will reward everyone for whatever good he does, whether he is slave or free."
- 1 Timothy 6:18–19, "Command them to do good, to be rich in good deeds, and to be generous and willing to share. In this way

they will lay up treasure for themselves as a firm foundation for the coming age, so that they may take hold of the life that is truly life."

While many of the above verses deal with rewards in the age to come, there is a sense that believers experience a foretaste of these rewards now. Jesus said that he came so we might have life and have it to the full (John 10:10) and, while this includes life in the new heaven and new earth, it also includes life now. We have a foretaste of the age to come now and enjoy a certain dimension of eternal life now.

The concept of rewards is also discussed in 1 Corinthians 3:10–15, "By the grace God has given me, I laid a foundation as an expert builder, and someone else is building on it. But each one should be careful how he builds. For no one can lay any foundation other than the one already laid, which is Jesus Christ. If any man builds on this foundation using gold, silver, costly stones, wood, hay or straw, his work will be shown for what it is, because the Day will bring it to light. It will be revealed with fire, and the fire will test the quality of each man's work. If what he has built survives, he will receive his reward. If it is burned up, he will suffer loss; he himself will be saved, but only as one escaping through the flames."

The day, that is the judgment day, will reveal the quality and quantity of our Christian service. Gold, silver, and costly stones represent service of value from a right motive, whereas wood, hay, or straw refers to service done from selfish motives or service of little value. Verse 15 reminds us that this judgment doesn't determine our eternal destiny, but simply our reward: "If it is burned up, he will suffer loss; he himself will be saved, but only as one escaping through the flames." Such a person will be saved but they will have little reward, something that Paul describes as "suffering loss." This passage suggests that there are degrees of reward, a subject that I will discuss shortly.

JUDGMENT WILL INCREASE OUR GRATITUDE TO GOD

While the primary purpose of judgment for believers is to reward them for Christian service, I believe that it also has the secondary purpose of showing us how great our sin was and how magnificent God's grace and love is. First Corinthians 4:5 tells us that judgment will go beyond what we said and did, for God will even reveal our motives. Nothing will be hidden: "Therefore judge nothing before the appointed time; wait till the Lord comes. He will bring to light what is hidden in darkness and will expose the motives of men's hearts. At that time each will receive his praise from God."

I suspect that most Christians, while they will happily admit that they are not perfect, really think that they are "not too bad," and are likely to think that God is obligated to accept them into heaven. It never ceases to amaze me how some born-again pastors think this way. When they talk about salvation they readily accept that people are saved by grace rather than works, but when they talk about church discipline they frequently demand godly behavior from their members because God will "not allow sinners into heaven." I have heard pastors use those exact words. On the surface, they believe that we are saved by faith and not because we are "good enough," but deep down, they have this thinking that says that we only make it into heaven because we are "good enough." As a result of this, they often become "self-righteous" in behavior.

When we stand before the throne of God and are judged by what we have done, we will suddenly realize that we are not even close to being accepted by God because of our works and that we deserve nothing but punishment. We will realize that we sin in many ways. For example:

- We sin because much of what we do is not from faith, but our own reasoning. (Rom 14:23)

- We do not continually glorify God or give thanks to him. We take much for granted, and often complain about the situations we are in. (Rom 1:21)

- We often do things in ministry because we are self-seeking; we want others to notice us and think about how spiritual we are. (Rom 2:8) We are sometimes motivated by selfish ambition. (Gal 5:20)

- We can be jealous of other people and the success they are having. (Gal 5:20)

- Some people rob God by not tithing. (Mal 3:8) Even some pastors try to justify it by saying that they earn very little money and are serving God, so therefore they don't have to give at least 10 percent, or whatever the Spirit is asking them to give.

However, when we discover that we have been forgiven, and that God welcomes us with open arms, we will be overwhelmed by his love and realize for the very first time the magnitude of his grace toward us. It is when we fully understand the reality of God's mercy that we will want to worship him in a way that we never thought possible. We will be filled with a gratitude that is beyond anything we can understand at the moment. Fortunately, we will have all eternity to praise and worship him.

REWARDS WILL BE BASED ON OUR FAITHFULNESS

Jesus' parable of the Talents in Matthew 25:14–30 gives us further insight into the final judgment. The first two servants are believers who set out to please their master by serving him, while the third servant can be seen as an unbeliever, for he had a wrong view of his master (Matt 25:24). This wrong view proves that he didn't know his master well, and therefore didn't want to serve him.

It is interesting to note that when the servants were judged, the first two servants received the same reward, since they had both used what they had been given and were faithful with it. Both generated 100 percent return, even though one earned double the amount of the other. Everyone has been born with different natural talents or abilities, and every person was given different spiritual gifts when he or she was born again and filled with the Spirit. God is going to judge us on how we used what he gave us rather than on how we compare with some of the world's most famous Christians. I will not be judged by the standard of what Billy Graham or Paul Yonggi Cho has achieved, but I will be judged on what I achieved with what God has given me and called me to do. I believe that a "two talent" person, who earns another two talents, will receive a greater reward than a "five talent" person who only gains four talents.

The concept that there will be degrees of rewards for believers is an interesting one, for how can people receive different rewards but still be absolutely happy in heaven? We need to understand that there will be no such thing as envy or jealousy in heaven to cause us to resent another person for having more than us. I, for one, will be quite happy for those who have been martyred for their faith to have a greater reward than me. However, I do think it is possible for people to experience varying degrees of appreciation of God but at the same time be happy.

Let me give an illustration from my own life concerning food, although it is a very poor illustration. I have always liked food, but because I was raised in a working-class environment, my culinary experiences were very limited, and so I enjoyed my grilled sausages and well-done steak with great delight. However, as I grew and started to travel around the world, I was exposed to different food, and so my tastes developed. I would now reject food that I enjoyed immensely in my youth as being totally unappetizing. This change in taste has both a negative and positive side to it. For example, if food is not up to my standard, then I can taste the difference and am disappointed with what I am eating, but when it is superbly prepared, it is a joy beyond anything I could have experienced in my "pre-enlightened" days. In both phases of life I was completely happy with my food—assuming it was prepared how I liked it at the time—but I now have a far greater appreciation of excellent food than I did previously.

I think the same applies to eternity. Every believer will be happy, but I suggest that those who appreciate God more now will appreciate him more in eternity, whereas those who only have a minimal relationship with God now will only have a lesser appreciation in heaven. This may be what Paul means in 1 Corinthians 3:15 when he says that people whose works are poor quality (wood, hay, and straw) will be saved, but they will suffer loss. The loss is that, while they will be happy, they will not have the depth of appreciation that other believers will have, those whose works have been quality gold, silver, and costly stones.

REWARDS ARE AN INCENTIVE FOR GODLY LIVING

One of the things that surprised me as I looked at the verses that related to judgment was how often Paul sees judgment as an incentive for godly living. Consider the following:

- 2 Corinthians 5:9–10, "So we make it our goal to please him, whether we are at home in the body or away from it. For we must all appear before the judgment seat of Christ, that each one may receive what is due him for the things done while in the body, whether good or bad."
- Romans 14:12–13, "So then, each of us will give an account of himself to God. Therefore let us stop passing judgment on one

another. Instead, make up your mind not to put any stumbling block or obstacle in your brother's way."

- Colossians 3:23–24, "Whatever you do, work at it with all your heart, as working for the Lord, not for men, since you know that you will receive an inheritance from the Lord as a reward. It is the Lord Christ you are serving."

Hebrews 10:24–25 takes it one step further and tells us that we should actively encourage one another to love and do good works because of the day of judgment: "And let us consider how we may spur one another on toward love and good deeds. Let us not give up meeting together, as some are in the habit of doing, but let us encourage one another—and all the more as you see the Day approaching."

WHO IS THE JUDGE?

The Son is going to be the one who judges. Consider the following:

- Matthew 25:31–32, "When the Son of Man comes in his glory, and all the angels with him, he will sit on his throne in heavenly glory. All the nations will be gathered before him, and he will separate the people one from another as a shepherd separates the sheep from the goats."
- Acts 10:42, "He commanded us to preach to the people and to testify that he [Jesus] is the one whom God appointed as judge of the living and the dead."
- John 5:22, 27, "Moreover, the Father judges no one, but has entrusted all judgment to the Son . . . And he [the Father] has given him [the Son] authority to judge because he is the Son of Man."

The New Testament also tells us that God is the one who judges:

- Hebrews 12:23, "You have come to God, the judge of all men, to the spirits of righteous men made perfect."
- 2 Thessalonians 1:5a, "All this is evidence that God's judgment is right."
- Romans 14:10b, "For we will all stand before God's judgment seat."

The idea that the Son judges but that God judges should not confuse us, for the Son is fully God. Verses such as Romans 14:10, which refer to God's judgment seat, and 2 Corinthians 5:10, which talk about the judgment seat of Christ, should not surprise us either, since the Son is also fully God. Jesus is the one who is going to judge.

ANGELS WILL ALSO BE JUDGED

The angels who sinned will be punished: "For if God did not spare angels when they sinned, but sent them to hell, putting them into gloomy dungeons to be held for judgment" (2 Peter 2:4). Verses such as 1 Corinthians 6:3a suggest that righteous angels will also be judged, since the word "angel" usually refers to this group: "Do you not know that we will judge angels?" Maybe they will be judged so they can be rewarded for their service to God.

BELIEVERS WILL BE INVOLVED IN THE JUDGMENT PROCESS

As remarkable as it may seem, Scripture suggests that believers will be involved in the judgment process, "Do you not know that the saints will judge the world? And if you are to judge the world, are you not competent to judge trivial cases? Do you not know that we will judge angels?" (1 Cor 6:2–3). Some Bible scholars say that it will be the testimony of the believers in accepting Jesus that will be used to judge those who have rejected Christ, but that doesn't seem to do full justice to the passage. Paul is urging the Corinthian believers to settle their disputes among themselves by acting as judges rather than taking each other to a pagan court. Since he tells them that they are competent to judge trivial cases, the thrust of the passage suggests that believers will, in some way, be involved in the final judgment; they will be more than observers.

DISCUSSION ON MATTHEW 25:31–46; THE SHEEP AND THE GOATS

Before I discuss these verses, let me talk about the dispensational interpretation of this passage. It teaches that this judgment is different to the final judgment (The great white throne in Revelation 20:11), and that it determines which nations will be admitted into Christ's millennial kingdom and which will be excluded. The basis of admission is how the nations treat the nation of Israel for they, according to this interpretation, are Jesus' brothers. I cannot agree with this for the millennial reign of Christ is not mentioned in this passage. Instead, it clearly states that people—the masculine pronoun is used—will either be ushered into eternal fire prepared for the devil and his angels (verse 41), or ushered into eternal life (verse 46). This is exactly the same outcome of the final judgment that occurs at the great white throne in Revelation 20:11-15. It seems almost impossible to interpret Matthew 25:31-46 as referring to a different judgment from that in Revelation 20:11-15. Both passages are referring to the final judgment.

One of the difficulties of this Matthew 25:31-46 passage is that it suggests, on the surface, that the basis for receiving eternal life is our good deeds. This is contrary to Paul's teaching that no one will be justified by his works (Eph 2:8-9; Rom 3:20,28), and John's teaching in Revelation 20 that no one will escape the lake of fire because of his or her works. The only way to receive eternal life is to have our name in the Lamb's book of life, and we achieve this by believing in Jesus. When this happens we are no longer under the wrath of God, but have eternal life: "Whoever believes in the Son has eternal life, but whoever rejects the Son will not see life, for God's wrath remains on him" (John 3:36). We know from Ephesians 2:8-9 that we are not saved by works but by faith. All this points away from interpreting this passage as saying that some will earn eternal life because of their acts of kindness and some will be thrown into the eternal fire because they did not perform sufficient good deeds.

We need to understand that while we are not saved by good works, good works are always the evidence of our salvation. Paul, for example, summarized his message as, "I preached that they should repent and turn to God and prove their repentance by their deeds" (Acts 26:20). Paul was adamant that we are not saved by works of any kind, but if our faith is genuine then our repentance must be proved by good deeds. In Ephesians 2:8-9 Paul clearly tells us that we are saved by grace through faith and not by works, but, in the following verse, he goes on to say that we were created to do good works, "which God prepared in advance for us to do" (Eph 2:10). James reminds us that "faith without deeds is useless" (James 2:20), and that we can see if a person has faith by what he does (James 2:18). He then cites Abraham as an example of genuine faith. Abraham's work of offering his son Isaac showed that his faith was real.

James doesn't say that Abraham earned his salvation by good works, but instead that his "faith was made complete by what he did" (James 2:22). His faith was seen by his works. Faith is always proved by how we live.

Let us examine the use of the word "for" in Matthew 25: 35, so that we can understand its meaning more clearly: "For I was hungry and you gave me something to eat, I was thirsty and you gave me something to drink, I was a stranger and you invited me." I believe that we should understand the word "for" in this context, as referring to the evidence of salvation rather than the cause of salvation. For example, if I said, "It rained for the streets were wet," I would understand "for" as clearly referring to the evidence of rain and not the cause. If I wanted to convey the latter meaning I could say, "It rained for the atmospheric conditions were right." I believe it is consistent with the New Testament to understand the word "for" in verse 35 as referring to the evidence of salvation rather than the cause of salvation.

With the above in mind, how do we understand the basis for judgment in Matthew 25:31–46? The answer is found in verse 40 and how we understand "the least of these brothers of mine." There are three interpretations I will mention.

- First, it refers to the poor and disadvantaged in the world, since Jesus had a special ministry to these people.
- It refers to those who are physical Jews.
- Finally, Jesus' brothers were his disciples, and how people received the disciples is an indication of how they received Jesus and his message.

I think the third interpretation has more appeal. We know that Jesus referred to his disciples as his "brothers and sisters" (Matt. 12:47–50). When Jesus sent out the seventy-two, he gave them instructions about what to do if the people in a town didn't accept them. He said, "He who listens to you listens to me; he who rejects you rejects me; but he who rejects me rejects him who sent me" (Luke 10:16). Accepting Jesus' brothers–his disciples and all believers–is the same as accepting Jesus and his message. Doing "good" to the followers of Jesus was usually a sign that a person had accepted the message of Jesus and had put his or her faith in him. First John 3:14 tells us that we know we have passed from death to life because we love our brothers.

Concerning the first interpretation that Jesus' brothers are the poor and disadvantaged, I firmly believe that God is passionate about the welfare of these people. James 1:27 reminds us that, "Religion that God our Father accepts as pure and faultless is this: to look after orphans and widows in their distress and to keep oneself from being polluted by the world." I do believe that part of the reward that a believer receives on the day of judgment will be based on how committed he or she has been to the welfare of these vulnerable people in our society. Likewise we should also be people who have a love for the physical Jew, not that we approve of everything the Israeli government does, but we should love these people; they are still God's chosen race and there will be a time when all Israel will be saved (Rom 11:26).

While part of our reward may be based on how we have treated the poor and disadvantaged and how we have treated the Jew, our salvation is not based on this. If it was, then it would be salvation by works rather than by faith alone. We are saved by accepting the message of Jesus and his disciples; these people are "his brothers."

We note that this passage refers to the final judgment and the basis on which we will be either admitted to eternal life or assigned to eternal fire. People will be judged on how they have responded to Jesus and his teaching, the evidence of which will be seen in their good works to others, especially to their fellow believers.

COMMENTS ON ROMANS 2:5–16

> But because of your stubbornness and your unrepentant heart, you are storing up wrath against yourself for the day of God's wrath, when his righteous judgment will be revealed. God "will give to each person according to what he has done." To those who by persistence in doing good seek glory, honor and immortality, he will give eternal life. But for those who are self-seeking and who reject the truth and follow evil, there will be wrath and anger. There will be trouble and distress for every human being who does evil: first for the Jew, then for the Gentile; but glory, honor and peace for everyone who does good: first for the Jew, then for the Gentile. (Rom 2:5–10)

These are verses that people sometimes use to support their view that salvation is based on our good works. However, the first thing we need to note is the context. This passage is in the segment of the letter where

Paul is arguing that everyone has sinned and has come short of what God expects. As a result of this, they deserve death. The summary statement of this section is found in Romans 3:20, "Therefore no one will be declared righteous in his sight by observing the law; rather, through the law we become conscious of sin." He then writes in verse 28, "For we maintain that a man is justified by faith apart from observing the law." It can't be made any clearer than this. Paul is not going to contradict himself in Romans 2:7 with something that is different from the theme of his argument that we are justified by faith apart from good works.

Note that Romans 2:5–16 does not say that we will get eternal life if our good deeds outweigh our bad, or anything like that. Note also that verse 8 tells us that there will be wrath and anger for everyone who is self-seeking. We need to look at these verses as a whole, and when we do, we realize that Paul is saying that if we persist in doing good and never sin, then God will give us eternal life. This is impossible to achieve. Surely no one would want to say that there has never been a moment in their life when he or she was self-seeking or never did some form of evil. The fact is that there are times when we are all self-seeking and follow evil; it is only a matter of degree that separates one person from another. We are all guilty and the Bible confirms it, "all have sinned and fall short of the glory of God" (Rom 3:23). The outcome of this self-seeking is eternal death (Rom. 6:23) or, to put it another way, "wrath, anger, trouble and distress" (Rom 2:8–9). Paul teaches the same thing in Galatians 3:10–11. He tells us that if we don't do everything that the law of God commands all the time, we are under a curse. We have previously noted that James also taught that if we break the law in one point, and he uses the example of the sin of showing favoritism to the rich over the poor, then we are guilty of breaking all of God's laws: "For whoever keeps the whole law and yet stumbles at just one point is guilty of breaking all of it" (James 2:10).

In summary, Romans 2:7–11 tells us that if we continually do good and never sin in any way, then God will give us eternal life. No one has ever been in this situation because we have all sinned at some stage in our life. We have all come short of the glory of God. Verse 6 reminds us that judgment is based on what we have done. It is not based on our background, whether we were born a Jew or into a Christian family, nor is it based on what others have done to us, circumcision or infant baptism or infant dedication, but on what we have done. The context of this passage tells us that when we are judged by our works, our deeds will confirm that we are sinners and deserve eternal death. Judgment is not to ascertain if our good deeds outweigh our bad, but to confirm that we haven't obeyed God's law every moment of every day. As James tells us, if we keep the whole law but break it in just one point, we are a law-breaker.

8

Hell

INTRODUCTION

THE IDEA OF HELL is not popular today, and many seem to have stopped preaching about it. However, it is an important part of biblical teaching, and we are disobedient to our calling as preachers if we ignore it. We need to warn people.

Anyone who has ever tried to witness to the Jehovah's Witnesses will know that they do not believe in hell. They say, "God is a God of love and wouldn't throw anyone into a fire. You wouldn't throw your children into a lake of fire, so why would God?" However, when we really think about it, we realize that this is based more on sentimentalism than anything else and has no biblical or rational basis. God is a God of love, but love demands justice, and justice demands punishment, and punishment demands a hell.

Consider the following. I read an article in a newspaper about the Russian mafia who were offering young women the opportunity to travel to a Mediterranean country and be employed in a modern office doing secretarial work. However, when the women arrived in the country, the mafia took them to a small apartment where they were held as prisoners and forced into continual prostitution. The women's passports were confiscated, and if they tried to escape, they were thrown from the apartment balcony and killed as a warning to others. Let us assume that the mafia bosses used their considerable wealth and power to bribe corrupt officials so that they could continue to avoid prosecution and live a life of absolute wealth and self-centered pleasure. Let us also assume that this continued until they died of old age. What would a God of love do to them on the day of judgment?

I have shared this story with many pastors and their response has always been the same as mine—one of righteous anger toward those men that they could abuse those girls and get away with it. None of us had ever met these women, but a love for them caused us to demand that justice be done. Love demands justice, and justice demands punishment for people who have committed such evil. A life in hell is the appropriate response from God toward those men. If God allows them to get away with what they have done to innocent women without punishing them, then God is either indifferent to people's hurts or powerless to do anything about it. I submit that he is neither. Hell is necessary if we have a God who is both powerful and loving.

Let me say that it is not our task to decide who God will send to hell and who he won't; we should simply preach the gospel message and leave those things in his hands.

THE REALITY OF HELL

Jesus referred to hell on numerous occasions.

- Matthew 5:22, "But I tell you that anyone who is angry with his brother will be subject to judgment. Again, anyone who says to his brother, 'Raca,' is answerable to the Sanhedrin. But anyone who says, 'You fool!' will be in danger of the fire of hell."

- Matthew 5:29, "If your right eye causes you to sin, gouge it out and throw it away. It is better for you to lose one part of your body than for your whole body to be thrown into hell."

- Matthew 10:28, "Do not be afraid of those who kill the body but cannot kill the soul. Rather, be afraid of the One who can destroy both soul and body in hell."

The Greek word that is translated "hell" is *geenna*, which is a transliteration of the Hebrew *Ge Hinnom*, which is the Valley of Hinnom. This valley was immediately southeast of Jerusalem and was basically the city garbage dump. This was where the people of Jerusalem brought their daily rubbish, as well as their dead animals, and even the bodies of criminals, if the criminals had no one else to bury them. A fire burned continually for sanitary purposes. Needless to say, the term "the Gehenna of fire" (the hell of fire), became a well-known term that conveyed the idea of something that was absolutely abhorrent. Jesus takes this well-known phrase to convey the idea that the eternal place of punishment is repugnant beyond belief.

Jesus also used other phrases to describe hell without the Greek word *geenna*. For example:

- Matthew 22:12–13, "'Friend,' he asked, 'how did you get in here without wedding clothes?' The man was speechless. Then the king told the attendants, 'Tie him hand and foot, and throw him outside, into the darkness, where there will be weeping and gnashing of teeth.'"
- Matthew 25:41, "Then he will say to those on his left, 'Depart from me, you who are cursed, into the eternal fire prepared for the devil and his angels.'"

The apostles also taught of the reality of hell, although they didn't use the Greek word *geenna*. One assumes that the picture of a continuously burning rubbish dump outside Jerusalem would not have carried much meaning for the Gentile world.

- Hebrews 10:26–27, "If we deliberately keep on sinning after we have received the knowledge of the truth, no sacrifice for sins is left, but only a fearful expectation of judgment and of raging fire that will consume the enemies of God."
- Jude 1:7, "In a similar way, Sodom and Gomorrah and the surrounding towns gave themselves up to sexual immorality and perversion. They serve as an example of those who suffer the punishment of eternal fire."
- Revelation 20:15, "If anyone's name was not found written in the book of life, he was thrown into the lake of fire."

THE WICKED ARE SENT TO HELL AT THE END OF THIS AGE

I have heard people say that there is no hell after we die for this life is hell. While one has to empathize with those who have been through horrendous times in this life, the Bible teaches that hell is a place that the wicked experience at the end of this age.

- Matthew 13:49–50, "This is how it will be at the end of the age. The angels will come and separate the wicked from the righteous

and throw them into the fiery furnace, where there will be weeping and gnashing of teeth."
- Revelation 20:11–13. These verses describe how the final judgment occurs at the end of this age, and that judgment leads immediately to hell for the unbeliever.

HELL: LITERAL OR SYMBOLIC FIRE

There are those who understand hell as containing literal fire, and many of the above verses are quoted to support this view. However, I feel that we should see the language of fire and flames as being symbolic rather than literal. For example, while Jesus refers to hell as fire he also refers to it as "darkness." Jude does the same in his letter, and refers to this place of eternal punishment as "eternal fire" (verse 7) and "blackest darkness" (verse 13). Literal fire and blackest darkness are mutually exclusive. However, if we understand these terms as being symbolic, then they help to paint a picture of the horror of hell.

Billy Graham, who apparently holds to the metaphorical view, made the following statement about the image of fire, "I have often wondered if hell is a terrible burning within our hearts for God, to fellowship with God, a fire that we can never quench."[1] I think that Billy Graham is on the right track in this regard. To be separated from all that is good, and to be in the company of total evil with only remorse for lost opportunities, would be hell; it doesn't need literal flames to make it sound horrific. To be without any hope for a better future, and to be surrounded by nothing but evil, would be "the final straw" of despair.

In summary, I believe that hell does not consist of literal physical fire. I believe that Jesus and the apostles use the word "fire" as a descriptive way to portray the pain and torment of hell; it is the best that they could do with their limited language and understanding.

Hell is Eternal

Scripture talks about hell as being eternal.
- Matthew 25:41, "Then he will say to those on his left, 'Depart from me, you who are cursed, into the eternal fire prepared for the devil and his angels.'"

---

1. Quoted in Crockett, *Four Views on Hell*, 45.

- Mark 9:43, "If your hand causes you to sin, cut it off. It is better for you to enter life maimed than with two hands to go into hell, where the fire never goes out."
- Matthew 3:12, "His winnowing fork is in his hand, and he will clear his threshing floor, gathering his wheat into the barn and burning up the chaff with unquenchable fire."

There are some who maintain that hell will eventually vanish because God can't be "all in all" if there is still a group of beings who are rebellious to his rule. (1 Cor 15:28 and other verses are used to support this concept.) However, I do not find these arguments convincing. Eternal means "forever and ever," rather than something which has a definite end, and I believe the Bible teaches that the "flames" of hell will continue for all eternity.

WHO GOES TO HELL?

There are two basic groups who will populate hell. The first group comprises the devil and his angels. Note the following:

- Matthew 25:41, "Then he will say to those on his left, 'Depart from me, you who are cursed, into the eternal fire prepared for the devil and his angels.'"
- 2 Peter 2:4, "For if God did not spare angels when they sinned, but sent them to hell, putting them into gloomy dungeons to be held for judgment . . .'"
- Revelation 20:10, "And the devil, who deceived them, was thrown into the lake of burning sulfur, where the beast and the false prophet had been thrown. They will be tormented day and night for ever and ever."

The second group who will populate hell are those who have rejected God, and who do not have their names written in the Lamb's book of life.

- Revelation 20:15, "If anyone's name was not found written in the book of life, he was thrown into the lake of fire."
- 2 Thessalonians 1:8–10a, "He will punish those who do not know God and do not obey the gospel of our Lord Jesus. They will be punished with everlasting destruction and shut out from the pres-

ence of the Lord and from the majesty of his power on the day he comes to be glorified in his holy people."

It is important to note that God didn't prepare hell for people, but, if they continue to rebel against him, he has no option but to send them there. God has given human beings the power to make basic choices that have eternal consequences. They can choose to follow him or to reject him. God does not save people against their will, and the existence of hell shows us how seriously God takes this gift of freedom. I love this statement from Zachary J. Hayes, "Hell is a necessary implication of human freedom."[2]

ETERNAL PUNISHMENT—NO SECOND CHANCE

I believe that punishment has two dimensions to it.

- First, a person will be punished according to what he or she has done (Rom 2:5–6). I have no idea how God is going to do this. I don't know whether he actively punishes people, or whether he withdraws his presence so that people are removed from any influence of good and are surrounded by evil. However, I know that Scripture teaches that people will be punished for their sin.

- The second aspect of punishment doesn't center around the punishment they receive, but rather what they are deprived of. Paul tells us in 2 Thessalonians 1:8–10a that the unbeliever will be shut out from the presence of God forever. There will be no second chance: "He will punish those who do not know God and do not obey the gospel of our Lord Jesus. They will be punished with everlasting destruction and shut out from the presence of the Lord and from the majesty of his power on the day he comes to be glorified in his holy people." These verses tell us that punishment will involve everlasting destruction where nonbelievers are deprived access to the presence of God. It seems that Paul's main concern is that unbelievers will not have a second chance to know God after they die; they will be shut out of his presence and will never experience the joy of being with him.

Down through the history of the church, people have suggested that God, because of his great love and mercy, will eventually save all

---

2. Quoted in Crockett, ed., *Four Views on Hell*, 128.

people. This is called universalism. Origen (c. AD 185–254) is probably the most famous advocate of this position. Such people often quote verses like Colossians 1:19 to support their view: "For God was pleased to have all his fullness dwell in him, and through him to reconcile to himself all things, whether things on earth or things in heaven, by making peace through his blood, shed on the cross." They see the lake of fire as purifying the sinner so that he can be accepted into the presence of God. This is reading too much into the text and totally changes the concept of salvation.

HELL CONSISTS OF CONSCIOUS TORMENT

Some theologians have advocated the idea that when the unbeliever is thrown into the lake of fire, which is the second death, he or she is immediately annihilated and there will be no such thing as conscious torment in hell. However, this doesn't do justice to what Jesus teaches.

- Matthew 13:49–50, "This is how it will be at the end of the age. The angels will come and separate the wicked from the righteous and throw them into the fiery furnace where there will be weeping and gnashing of teeth." This clearly refers to the final judgment when the unbeliever is thrown into the lake of fire. Note that there will be weeping and gnashing of teeth in the lake of fire, which shows that the wicked are consciously enduring torment in hell. Jesus uses this terminology six times in the book of Matthew, so it is not an isolated thought (Matt 8:12; 13:42; 22:13; 24:51; 25:30).

- Matthew 10:14–15, "If anyone will not welcome you or listen to your words, shake the dust off your feet when you leave that home or town. I tell you the truth, it will be more bearable for Sodom and Gomorrah on the day of judgment than for that town." If every wicked person has the same fate —that is, immediate annihilation in the lake of fire without any conscious torment—then how could it be more bearable on the day of judgment for the wicked inhabitants of Sodom than for the citizens who rejected the teaching of Jesus? If the wicked endure conscious torment in hell, then the words of Jesus are very clear.

- The concept of the justice of God leads us to believe in a hell where the wicked endure some form of torment for their rebellion. The idea that a person can deliberately rebel against God, and cause untold suffering to others because of their deliberate sin, and not have to suffer for it, doesn't seem right.

DEGREES OF TORMENT IN HELL

I have deliberately used the term "degrees of torment in hell" rather than "degrees of punishment." Punishment is eternal, for the unbeliever is shut out from the presence of God and is not given a second change. In this sense, every unbeliever suffers the same degree of punishment regardless of what they did on earth. However, the Bible talks about degrees of "torment" in hell; for the want of a better word.

- Matthew 10:15, "I tell you the truth, it will be more bearable for Sodom and Gomorrah on the day of judgment than for that town." The whole concept of punishment being more bearable for one group than another, suggests that there will be degrees of suffering in hell.

- Matthew 11:22, "But I tell you, it will be more bearable for Tyre and Sidon on the day of judgment than for you."

It is difficult to know how God is going to achieve this for we are talking about events that are hard for us to grasp with our finite minds. While Scripture doesn't give us any detail on how it will be "more bearable" for one person than another, one can imagine that the pain level could be increased or decreased or that the duration of consciousness in hell could be lengthened or shortened accordingly. (The second suggestion impinges on the issue of eternal conscious punishment and the immortality of the human soul as per the following discussion.)

ETERNAL CONSCIOUS PUNISHMENT?

Introduction

The Bible tells us that the unbeliever will be punished eternally so that there is no second chance to be saved. We have noted that such a person is not taken to heaven after he has purified himself by enduring the torment of hell for a period of "time," nor is he immediately annihilated after being thrown into the lake of fire so that there is no conscious torment in hell. While hell is eternal punishment, and while he will experience pain that results in "weeping and gnashing of teeth," we need to ask if hell is eternal conscious punishment; that is, will the unbeliever be consciously aware of torment and pain for ever and ever without end.

The traditional view, but not necessarily the biblical view, is that the unbeliever will be fully conscious and that he will feel the pain and anguish of hell for all eternity. This view is usually based on the assumption that man has an immortal soul that cannot die. You may have heard the preacher say, "It is not a matter of if you will live forever, but where will you live. Man has an eternal soul and will therefore live forever; it is only a matter of where: heaven or hell."

Is this right? Do people have immortal souls? Will they live forever because their souls are immortal? Let me say that I am not asking if a person's soul/spirit will live on after physical death, because it will, but does a person contain immortality within himself; is his soul incapable of death? This has a major bearing on our discussion, because I have never heard a preacher advocate that God deliberately torments a person forever and ever in hell because God chooses to do so. The reason given for eternal conscious punishment is usually that the unbeliever has an immortal soul, and therefore has to consciously live forever in hell; God doesn't choose to do this but he has no other option.

I believe that this teaching of the "immortality of the soul" came into the church as more and more Greek-thinking people were saved; they, like all of us, brought their worldly philosophies with them and reinterpreted the Scripture in light of them. Greek philosophy taught that man's soul was immortal and his body evil, so that salvation was the escape of the immortal soul from the confines of the body. I believe that the doctrine of the immortality of the soul is pagan Greek thinking and not biblical teaching.

Does a Person Have an Immortal Soul?

Before I answer this question, I want to make it clear that I am not asking if the soul of a person survives physical death, for the Bible plainly teaches that it does. However, we must not interpret this continuation of the soul after death to mean that it is immortal. Immortality means that the soul is incapable of dying. The fact that the soul survives physical death doesn't mean that it is immortal; it simply means that it can survive without a physical body. While I was doing a final edit to this manuscript, I read a book where the author was strongly defending the immortality of the soul on the basis that it continued to live on even though the body had died. I believe that this is an invalid assumption.

Now for the question, "Is man's soul immortal?" I believe that the Bible teaches a very definite "No!" on this issue. Scripture tells us that only God is immortal: "God, the blessed and only Ruler, the King of kings and Lord of lords, who alone is immortal and who lives in unapproachable light, whom no one has seen or can see. To him be honor and might forever. Amen" (1 Tim 6:15b–16). Genesis 3:22–23 teaches that God took steps to prevent man having immortality while he was a sinner: "And the Lord God said, 'The man has now become like one of us, knowing good and evil. He must not be allowed to reach out his hand and take also from the tree of life and eat, and live forever.' So the Lord God banished him from the Garden of Eden to work the ground from which he had been taken." These are remarkable verses for they show the greatness of God's love towards us. God does not want man to live forever and ever in hell, and that is why he made it impossible for man to eat of the tree of life and gain immortality while he was a sinner.

The Wages of Sin is Death but the Gift of God is Eternal Life

I was raised in a church that taught that a person has an immortal soul, and would therefore suffer eternal conscious torment if he or she rejected Christ. However, there were a number of verses that puzzled me greatly as a teenager. One of them was Genesis 2:16–17, "And the Lord God commanded the man, 'You are free to eat from any tree in the garden; but you must not eat from the tree of the knowledge of good and evil, for when you eat of it you will surely die.'" Yes, man died spiritually when he ate of the fruit, and he started to die physically as a result of that act of disobedience, but if man has an immortal soul then the "real us," the inner person, his soul/spirit, does not die; yet Scripture says that he will die.

Verses like Romans 6:23 also puzzled me, "For the wages of sin is death, but the gift of God is eternal life in Christ Jesus our Lord." If the sinner lives forever in hell, then how can the wages of sin be death? The traditional view, which I was taught, understands Romans 6:23 as, "The wages of sin is eternal life in torment in hell, but the gift of God is eternal life in heaven." This is not how the verse reads.

I believe that we are meant to take the above verses exactly as they read. The wages of sin is death and this occurred in three stages:

- When Adam and Eve sinned, they, and all their descendants, died spiritually—that is, they lost spiritual life and spiritual consciousness.
- We also die physically—that is, we lose bodily life and bodily consciousness.
- Finally, the soul of the sinner will die—that is, he or she will lose all form of "inner life" and have no conscious existence at all.

Death by definition is the cessation of life; we will no longer have any consciousness.

The ultimate fate of the unbeliever is destruction, which is another way of saying, "death."

- Matthew 10:28, "Do not be afraid of those who kill the body but cannot kill the soul. Rather, be afraid of the One who can destroy both soul and body in hell."
- 2 Thessalonians 1:8–9, "He will punish those who do not know God and do not obey the gospel of our Lord Jesus. They will be punished with everlasting destruction and shut out from the presence of the Lord and from the majesty of his power."
- 2 Peter 3:7, "By the same word the present heavens and earth are reserved for fire, being kept for the day of judgment and destruction of ungodly men."

When chaff is thrown into a fire it is burnt up and destroyed. An eternal hell does not mean that a person will be conscious forever, but that, after a period of appropriate torment, he or she will be destroyed and will, therefore, die.

The second half of Romans 6:23 tells us that eternal life is a gift. Again, we should understand this exactly as it reads; eternal life, the ability to live forever and ever, is a gift from God. God, in his love, only gives this gift to people who repent of their sin and are born again. We noted in Genesis 3:22–24 that God placed cherubim at the entrance to the garden to stop sinners from eating of the tree of life. In the book of Revelation, the tree appears again, but this time it is freely available to those who wash their robes—to those who have been cleansed of their sin because of their faith in Christ: "Blessed are those who wash their robes, that they may have the right to the tree of life and may go through the gates into the city" (Rev 22:14).

We receive this gift of eternal life, or immortality, in two stages:

- First, when we are born again, we receive eternal life, and therefore our soul/spirit will live forever.

- Then, at the second coming of Christ, we will receive our immortal resurrection body that will also live forever: "Listen, I tell you a mystery: We will not all sleep, but we will all be changed—in a flash, in the twinkling of an eye, at the last trumpet. For the trumpet will sound, the dead will be raised imperishable, and we will be changed. For the perishable must clothe itself with the imperishable, and the mortal with immortality. When the perishable has been clothed with the imperishable, and the mortal with immortality, then the saying that is written will come true: 'Death has been swallowed up in victory'" (1 Cor 15:51–54).

This concept that I am advocating is sometimes called "conditional immortality," because we receive immortality only on the condition that we are born again.

Eternal Conscious Punishment in Church History

In his book *The Problem of Immortality*, published in London in 1892, E. Petavel looks at the early Church Fathers to ascertain whether they were "conditionalists" (sin results in death; the view I am advocating), "traditionalists" (eternal conscious torment), or "universalists" (everyone will eventually be saved as a result of the purifying nature of hell).[3] He concludes that the early Church Fathers—Barnabas, Clement of Rome, Ignatius, the author of the Didache, Hermas, Polycarp, and Justin—were all conditionalists, although there were elements of other positions in the writings of Justin. After this period of time, the traditionalists appeared and then the universalists. If the above is true, then it confirms that the New Testament church did not believe in eternal conscious punishment, but it was introduced into Christian theology as the influence of Greek philosophy crept into the church.

Not all accept the above as being correct, but see the traditional view as being the view of the Bible. William Crockett also quotes from Clement, Polycarp, and others to support his view of eternal conscious punishment.[4] However, I do not think his conclusions are correct. For

---

3. Forster, *Heaven and Hell*, 29, quoting E. Petavel, *The Problem of Immortality*.
4. Crockett, *Four views on Hell*, 65–66.

example, he quotes the *Epistle of Diognetius* as referring to "those that shall be condemned to the everlasting fire"; 2 Clement as reading, "nothing shall rescue us from eternal punishment"; *The Martydom of Polycarp*, which refers to, "the fire which is everlasting and is never quenched," and "the fire which awaits the wicked in the judgment to come and in everlasting punishment." I certainly do not deny that the fire of hell is everlasting or that punishment is eternal, but I do not believe that this means eternal conscious torment.

Plato's Use of the Greek Language

I am advocating that the unbelieving sinner does not have immortality within him, and he or she only receives immortality as a gift from God when he repents and is born again. However, Plato and other Greek philosophers held to a different view and believed that a man's soul was immortal and incapable of death. If this is so, then we should expect to see a difference in the way the New Testament writers used various Greek words to that of the Greek philosophers. I believe that we do see this difference when we compare the two. Roger Forster, in his booklet, *Heaven and Hell: man's eternal destiny,* says that Plato used the Greek words for "death," "perishing," "corruption," "destruction," and "die" in his writings, and said that the soul was not subject to any of them, because it would live forever. The New Testament, on the other hand, applies all these words to the lost soul and says that it is subject to them and will die.[5] This is a strong argument to support the concept that Jesus and the apostles taught that a person's soul was not immortal and would be destroyed in hell and ultimately lose all consciousness.

I'M NOT TAKING THE "HELL" OUT OF HELL

The criticism that is sometimes directed against what I am saying is that I have taken the hell out of hell; I have reduced its horror. Let me respond by making a number of points:

- My intention is to find out what Jesus and his apostles taught about hell. We do that by reading the New Testament, which is the inspired, infallible word of God. If what I am suggesting is different to what we have been traditionally taught, then so be it.

---

5. Forster, *Heaven and Hell*, 28.

The Bible, not church tradition, is our ultimate source of authority in all matters relating to faith and conduct.

- This view still has a large scope for the "horror of hell." There is no reason why people could not spend the equivalent of say ten thousand years or more in hell before they were burnt up and destroyed. God is the judge, and he will decide what is just. We can rely on God to do what is right.

- I can't remember the last time I went to church and heard a pastor preach on hell. This makes me wonder if Christians really do believe in hell anymore. The horror of hell as eternal conscious punishment doesn't seem to motivate evangelical and Pentecostal pastors to teach it. One has to ask, why! Do they have such reservations about the justice of God in assigning people to eternal conscious punishment, especially those who have never heard the gospel, that they can't bring themselves to preach about it?

WHAT ABOUT THOSE WHO HAVE NEVER HEARD THE GOSPEL?

One of the difficult questions that people ask is, "What will God do to the person who hasn't heard the gospel?" I have heard people maintain that God will take those who have never heard to heaven, since they have not had an opportunity to reject Christ. There is nothing in the Bible that teaches this. If this was true, then we should stop obeying the Great Commission immediately and not send any missionaries to unreached people groups, for the moment they hear the gospel they will be doomed to hell rather than going to heaven. This teaching is ridiculous, but it is understandable, because we don't want to see "nice" people being assigned to a life of eternal conscious torment in hell when they have never had the opportunity to hear the gospel and repent.

One of the many flaws of the above argument is that it assumes that the basis for being sent to hell is whether we have accepted Christ or not. This is not true. We will be sent to hell because we have sinned and our life has not come up to the standard of God's holy perfection. It is true that if we turn to Christ in repentance and faith we will be saved from hell, but failure to do this is not the reason we are sent to hell; we are sent to hell because we are sinners.

However, there is a second view that I want to comment on. There are some Bible-believing scholars who advocate that when someone who has never heard the gospel looks into nature and understands from it, and from his own conscience, that there has to be a holy God and that he doesn't come up to this standard, if he repents of his ways and throws himself on the mercy of this God in faith, then God will give him eternal life at the day of judgment. This view is different to the first one, for it takes sin seriously and it understands that we can only be saved by repentance and faith based on what Christ has done. It is true that we do not have to understand the grounds on which we are acquitted of our sin in order to be saved, for the Old Testament saints didn't have to fully understand the death and resurrection of Christ in order to benefit from it.

When I first heard this argument it helped me to understand more about the justice and love of God, as well as the nature of salvation. Up to this time I had a very hard and legalistic view of God and was sure you couldn't get into heaven unless you had literally said the "sinner's prayer." Fortunately, I changed my thinking when I became a pastor and saw how God genuinely saved people under different circumstances. However, while this is an interesting theory and has some merit to it, we have to be careful not to say that it is what the New Testament teaches. What is clear from Scripture is that we have been commanded to go into all the world and make disciples of all nations. We have to obey what we have been told to do and leave the eternal destiny of such people to God, who we can be assured, will do what is right.

SUMMARY

Let me summarize this teaching:

- There is a hell that is eternal and will go on forever and ever.
- It is described as "fire" and "utter darkness." As these two concepts are mutually exclusive, I see these words as being symbolic. They are word pictures to describe the horror of hell.
- It was prepared for the devil and his angels, but sadly, those who reject Jesus will also be sent there. This is determined at the final judgment.

- Hell is eternal punishment. By that I mean there is no second chance to get right with God and go to heaven. The unbeliever is shut out of the presence of God forever. This punishment will continue forever.
- There are degrees of torment in hell.
- The wages of sin is death. This means that after an appropriate amount of suffering the soul of a person dies. The person ceases to have conscious existence even though they are still in the "fire of hell."

9

The New Heaven and New Earth

THE BELIEVER'S FINAL DESTINY IS THE NEW HEAVEN AND NEW EARTH

I GREW UP WITH the belief, one that seems to be common among some Bible-believing Christians, that the final destiny for the believer is heaven, and that heaven is a place somewhere up in the sky. This is not exactly true, for our final destiny is the new heaven and new earth, and this is what we are to look forward to.

- Isaiah 65:17, "Behold, I will create new heavens and a new earth. The former things will not be remembered, nor will they come to mind."

- 2 Peter 3:13, "But in keeping with his promise we are looking forward to a new heaven and a new earth, the home of righteousness."

- Revelation 21:1–3, "Then I saw a new heaven and a new earth, for the first heaven and the first earth had passed away, and there was no longer any sea. I saw the Holy City, the new Jerusalem, coming down out of heaven from God, prepared as a bride beautifully dressed for her husband. And I heard a loud voice from the throne saying, 'Now the dwelling of God is with men, and he will live with them. They will be his people, and God himself will be with them and be their God.'"

I think that the concept of our final destiny being somewhere "up in the sky," rather than on a renewed earth, is something that we have absorbed from Greek philosophy, especially that of Plato. For the Greeks, the spirit was pure and salvation was an escape of the soul from the body, which was seen by some as evil, or at least restricting. For them, the spirit world was the real world, while the physical world was temporary, and only gave an appearance of reality. One's ultimate destiny was for the soul to be freed from the body and to live forever in the invisible spirit world. This is a view that is not all that different from what we hear preached in some of our churches. However, the biblical view is that man will live forever with God on a renewed earth with an immortal resurrection body.

HEAVEN COMES DOWN TO THE NEW EARTH AND THE TWO BECOME ONE

After the final judgment, the first heaven and first earth "pass away" and are renewed so that they become the new heaven and new earth (Rev 21:1-4). In Revelation 21:2, John sees the holy city, the dwelling of God, coming down to the new earth so that God is now living with his people. Heaven, the place where God's presence is centralized, has now come down to the renewed earth so that the two become one. This is the new heaven and new earth that people have looked forward to down through the ages (Isa 65:17; 2 Peter 3:13). This is where the believer, with his resurrection body, will spend eternity; he will be with God and will see him face to face (Rev 22:4). This is a picture of complete fellowship where nothing is hidden or restricted.

Revelation 21 describes the holy city, the dwelling place of God, in three ways.

- The holy city is the "New Jerusalem" (Rev 21:2), which is seen in the Bible as the dwelling place of God: "But you have come to Mount Zion, to the heavenly Jerusalem, the city of the living God. You have come to thousands upon thousands of angels in joyful assembly, to the church of the firstborn, whose names are written in heaven" (Heb 12:22-23a). In other words, the New Jerusalem is heaven, the place where God's presence is centered, and where Jesus sits at the right hand of the Father. In Revelation 21:2-3, the dwelling place of God—heaven—comes down to the renewed earth.

- The holy city is also the "people of God"—the "bride of Christ." Verse 2 tells us that the holy city is "prepared as a bride beautifully dressed for her husband." We see the same truth in verses

9-10: "One of the seven angels who had the seven bowls full of the seven last plagues came and said to me, 'Come, I will show you the bride, the wife of the Lamb.' And he carried me away in the Spirit to a mountain great and high, and showed me the Holy City, Jerusalem, coming down out of heaven from God." The angel said that he would show John the bride, the wife of the Lamb, and then proceeds to show him the holy city. The bride is the church, the people of God (Eph 5:25-32).

Some may ask why the believers are back in heaven if they have reigned with Christ on earth during the millennium. The answer is found in Revelation 20:11. The final judgment follows the millennium and everyone, including the saints in their resurrection bodies, must stand before the great white throne to be judged. Remember, the primary purpose of judgment for believers is to determine the rewards they will receive. They already know that they are accepted by God, for they have their resurrection bodies and have reigned with Christ.

- The holy city is also described in terms of the "Holy of Holies." In verse 9 the angel tells John that he will show him the wife of the bride, but shows him the holy city. The city is described as a cube; it is 12,000 stadia (2,200km) in length, and as wide and high as it is long. This cube configuration would have drawn the reader's attention to the Holy of Holies, which was also a perfect cube. The measurement of 12,000 stadia is not to be taken literally in this book of symbols, but is itself symbolic. It is 12 x 1000; 12 being the people of God, and 1000 being 10 x 10 x 10, the number of completion.

Note that the wall of the city has twelve foundations, which are the apostles of the Lamb, for the church is built on the apostles (Eph 2:20), and it has twelve gates, which are the tribes of Israel. Interestingly, the wall is 144 cubits wide or high, depending on how one translates the verse, which equals twelve times twelve and represents the people of God in the Old Covenant and the people of God in the New.

This concept of the holy city being described in terms of the Holy of Holies in the Old Testament should not surprise us, for the Holy of Holies was where the presence of God resided; nor should it surprise us that it also refers to the church. In 2 Corinthians 6:16

Paul tells us that, "we are the temple of the living God." God dwells in his church and he dwells in us. We are the bride of Christ.

There is no temple as such in the new heaven and new earth, for the Lord God almighty and the Lamb are its temple (verse 22); nothing else is needed.

It is interesting to note that the holy city is described in terms of a city of the first century, for that is what people in John's day could understand. Revelation 22:15 tells us that, "outside are the dogs, those who practice magic arts, the sexually immoral, the murderers, the idolaters, and everyone who loves and practices falsehood." We know from Revelation 20:11–15 that if anyone's name wasn't recorded in the Lamb's book of life they were thrown into the lake of fire. Therefore, the only people on the new heaven and new earth are those whose names are written in the Lamb's book of life, for the remainder have been banished to hell. However, Revelation is a book of symbols, and this symbol of the holy city as a first-century city helps us to understand the wonder of the new heaven and new earth; it is a place of safety and goodness.

As believers we are already citizens of this heavenly city, the New Jerusalem (heaven), even while we are living on this present earth: "But our citizenship is in heaven. And we eagerly await a Savior from there, the Lord Jesus Christ" (Phil 3:20). If the believer dies before the return of Christ, then heaven, or paradise, or the heavenly Jerusalem—whichever term one wishes to use—is the believer's dwelling place while he awaits his resurrection body and his final home on the new earth. God already has our citizenship papers with him, so we can be sure that we will be admitted into our new home.

IS IT A TOTALLY NEW EARTH OR THE PRESENT EARTH MADE NEW?

There is some difference of opinion among Bible scholars as to whether this existing earth will be completely destroyed and a new one created somewhere else, or if the present earth will be dramatically transformed so that it is renewed.

A casual glace at Revelation 21:1 and 2 Peter 3:10 suggests that our final destination is on a totally different earth: "Then I saw a new heaven and a new earth, for the first heaven and the first earth had passed away, and there was no longer any sea" (Rev 21:1). Refer also to 2 Peter 3:10,

"But the day of the Lord will come like a thief. The heavens will disappear with a roar; the elements will be destroyed by fire, and the earth and everything in it will be laid bare." However, I believe that the new earth will be this present earth, but dramatically renewed so that it is freed from any consequence of sin. Consider the following:

- Romans 8:19–21, "The creation waits in eager expectation for the sons of God to be revealed. For the creation was subjected to frustration, not by its own choice, but by the will of the one who subjected it, in hope that the creation itself will be liberated from its bondage to decay and brought into the glorious freedom of the children of God." These verses suggest that it is this present earth that will be liberated from its present state of decay and transformed into a new earth that is a fit home for believers.

- 2 Peter 3:10, as mentioned above, talks about the elements being destroyed by fire and everything in it being laid bare. This is probably referring to the same thing that Paul has in mind in Romans 8:19–21, and is a dramatic way of saying that this earth will be transformed and set free from the bondage that it currently experiences.

- I like Hedrickson's comment on Revelation 21:1, "Out of the great conflagration a new universe has been born. The word used in the original implies that it was a 'new' but not an 'other' world. It is the same heaven and earth, but gloriously rejuvenated, with no weeds, thorns or thistle, and so on. Nature comes into it own; all of its potentialities, dormant so long, are now fully realized."[1]

- The principle behind Romans 8:28 is another argument that supports the concept that God will transform the existing earth and make it new, rather than scrapping it and starting again. If it was a totally new earth, it might suggest that God doesn't have the power to take a creation, which was originally "very good" but damaged by sin, and renew it. The principle of Romans 8:28 is that God can take any situation that Satan brings against us and turn it around so that good results. I believe the same applies to creation. The present earth is not irretrievable because of the work of Satan, but can be renewed by the power of God. When the present earth is renewed it will show God's total victory and power over Satan.

---

1. Hendriksen, *More than Conquerors*, 198–99.

We need to understand John's comment concerning the sea in Revelation 21:1 as being symbolic rather than literal: "and there was no longer any sea." In this book of vivid pictures, the sea is the source of evil from which the beast comes (Rev 13:1). In the Old Testament it is a symbol of restlessness: "But the wicked are like the tossing sea, which cannot rest, whose waves cast up mire and mud" (Isa 57:20). Morris writes the following concerning Revelation 21:1, "We must moreover bear in mind that in antiquity people did not have the means for coping successfully with the sea's dangers and they regarded it as an unnatural element, a place of storms and danger."[2] This passage tells us that in the new heaven and new earth there will be no source of evil but only good; no vast expanse of restlessness but rather a deep inner fulfillment; no fear but a rewarding peace. We must not interpret this verse to teach that there will be no literal oceans or lakes or rivers in the new heaven and new earth; that would be to misunderstand the meaning of apocalyptic literature.

WHAT WILL WE DO THERE?

No Sorrow

Let me start by noting some of the things we will not be doing: "He will wipe every tear from their eyes. There will be no more death or mourning or crying or pain, for the old order of things has passed away" (Rev 21:4). Mourning, crying, and pain will be done away with, for these are the result of sin in the world. In Revelation 22:2 we see a reference to the "tree of life," although it is better to understand it as a "park of trees" rather than an individual tree.[3] This "park of trees" is a symbolic way of referring to the complete healing we will experience. There will no longer be any curse (verse 3), or any sickness, or war, or grieving, or injustice, for there will be complete healing from the consequences of sin. It doesn't matter how physically or emotional abused we may have been in this age, there will be total healing when we get to the new heaven and new earth. Our salvation will be complete.

---

2. Morris, *Revelation*, 237.
3. Hendriksen, *More than Conquerors*, 206.

Worship

A look at Revelation shows that we will worship God, for this seems to be a natural response to being in his presence.

- Revelation 4:9–10, "Whenever the living creatures give glory, honor and thanks to him who sits on the throne and who lives for ever and ever, the twenty-four elders fall down before him who sits on the throne, and worship him who lives for ever and ever."

- Revelation 5:11–12, "Then I looked and heard the voice of many angels, numbering thousands upon thousands, and ten thousand times ten thousand. They encircled the throne and the living creatures and the elders. In a loud voice they sang: 'Worthy is the Lamb, who was slain, to receive power and wealth and wisdom and strength and honor and glory and praise!'"

- Revelation 7:9–10, "After this I looked and there before me was a great multitude that no one could count, from every nation, tribe, people and language, standing before the throne and in front of the Lamb. They were wearing white robes and were holding palm branches in their hands. And they cried out in a loud voice: 'Salvation belongs to our God, who sits on the throne, and to the Lamb.'"

Serve God

We will serve God: "The throne of God and of the Lamb will be in the city, and his servants will serve him" (Rev 22:3b). The Greek word translated as "serve," has overtones of worship but seems to be slightly different. Heaven is not going to be a place where we will laze around wondering what to do with ourselves, feeling bored; rather we will be involved in serving God. Nor will it be a place of tension or weariness, for it is described as a place where we will rest from our labor: "Then I heard a voice from heaven say, 'Write: Blessed are the dead who die in the Lord from now on.' 'Yes,' says the Spirit, 'they will rest from their labor, for their deeds will follow them'" (Rev 14:13).

The new heaven and new earth will be a place of meaningful activity that results in us being called a "blessed people." It has been suggested that, since God is the origin of creativity, the most beautiful artwork that mankind has ever known will be painted there, along with the most moving music ever composed, and the most creative literature ever written. These things will surpass anything we have experienced on this present earth.

Fellowship With God and Each Other

The most important aspect of the new heaven and new earth is that God will be with his people and that we will "see his face" (Rev 22:4). We will experience intimate fellowship with God and with each other.

I am a person who loves good food with good friends. I find that these times of eating and sharing provide a deep satisfaction and enjoyment on many levels; it produces a fellowship that is hard to match. I do not find it a coincidence that the resurrection body is able to eat and drink (Acts 10:41), and that Revelation describes the union of Christ and his people in the new heaven and new earth as the "marriage supper of the Lamb." I believe that we will eat and drink with God and with each other, and therefore experience a fellowship and enjoyment beyond anything we have previously known. I also believe that the quality of the food will also be superior to what we now know.

CLOSING STATEMENT

I can't think of a better way to close this book than by quoting Revelation 22:12–13, 17, 20.

> "Behold, I am coming soon! My reward is with me, and I will give to everyone according to what he has done. I am the Alpha and the Omega, the First and the Last, the Beginning and the End."
>
> The Spirit and the bride say, "Come!" And let him who hears say, "Come!" Whoever is thirsty, let him come; and whoever wishes, let him take the free gift of the water of life.
>
> He who testifies to these things says, "Yes, I am coming soon." Amen. Come, Lord Jesus.

Bibliography

Barclay, William. *The Letters to the Philippians, Colossians, and Thessalonians.* Philadelphia, PA: Westminster, 1959.
Barker, Kenneth. *NIV Study Bible.* Grand Rapids: Zondervan, 1985.
Beasley-Murray, George. "2 Corinthians." In *The Broadman Bible Commentary*, edited by Clifton J. Allen, 11:1–76. Nashville: Broadman, 1971.
Bruce, F.F. *The Letter of Paul to the Romans.* Leicester: InterVarsity, 2003.
Clouse, Robert. *The Meaning of the Millennium: Four Views.* Downers Grove: InterVarsity, 1977.
Crockett, William, ed. *Four Views on Hell.* Grand Rapids: Zondervan, 1996.
Drummond, Lewis. *The Evangelist.* Nashville: Word Publishing, 2001.
Forster, Roger. *Heaven and Hell: Man's Eternal Destiny.* London: Ichthus Media, 1997.
Geldenhuys, Norval. *Commentary on the Gospel of Luke.* Grand Rapids: Eerdmans, 1975.
Grudem, Wayne. *Systematic Theology: An Introduction to Biblical Doctrine.* Leicester: InterVarsity, 1994.
Hendriksen, William. *More than Conquerors: An Interpretation of the Book of Revelation.* Grand Rapids: Baker, 1982
Hobbs, Herschel H. "Commentary on 1-2 Thessalonians." In *The Broadman Bible Commentary*, edited by Clifton J. Allen, 11:257–98. Nashville: Broadman, 1971.
Ladd, George. *A Commentary on the Revelation of John,* Grand Rapids: Eerdmans, 1978.
———. *The Last Things: An Eschatology for Laymen.* Grand Rapids: Eerdmans, 1978.
Lane, William. *The Gospel According to Mark.* Grand Rapids: Eerdmans, 1975.
Larkin, Clarence. *Dispensational Truth or God's Plan and Purpose in the Ages.* Philadelphia: Rev. Clarence Larkin Est., 1920
Morris, Leon. *The Book of Revelation.* Leicester: InterVarsity, 2004.
———. *The Epistles of Paul to the Thessalonians.* London: Tyndale, 1968.
———. *The Epistle to the Romans.* Grand Rapids: Eerdmans, 1997.
———. *The Gospel According to John.* Grand Rapids: Eerdmans, 1975.
———. *The Gospel According to Matthew.* Grand Rapids: Eerdmans, 1992.
———. *The Gospel According to St. Luke: An Introduction and Commentary.* Leicester: InterVarsity, 1976.
———. "The Antichrist." In *The New Bible Dictionary*, 39–40. Leicester: InterVarsity, 1976.
———. "Resurrection." In *The New Bible Dictionary*, 1086–89. Leicester: InterVarsity, 1976.
Mounce, Robert. *The Book of Revelation.* Grand Rapids: Eerdmans, 1977.

Petavel, E. *The Problem of Immortality.* Translated by Frederick Ash Freer. London: Elliot Stock, 1892.

Sproul, R.C. *The Last Days According to Jesus.* Grand Rapids: Baker, 2001.

Summers, Ray. *The Life Beyond.* Nashville: Broadman, 1959.

Tolbert, Malcolm O. "Luke." In *The Broadman Bible Commentary*, edited by Clifton J. Allen, 9:1–187, Nashville, Broadman, 1970.

Williams, J. Rodman. *Renewal Theology: Systematic Theology from a Charismatic Perspective.* 3 vols. in 1. Grand Rapids: Zondervan, 1996.

www.ingramcontent.com/pod-product-compliance
Lightning Source LLC
Chambersburg PA
CBHW072146160426
43197CB00012B/2268